BRIGHT NOTES

THE RAPE OF THE LOCK AND OTHER WORKS BY ALEXANDER POPE

Intelligent Education

Nashville, Tennessee

BRIGHT NOTES: The Rape of the Lock and Other Works
www.BrightNotes.com

No part of this publication may be used or reproduced in any manner whatsoever without written permission, except in the case of brief quotations in critical articles and reviews. For permissions, contact Influence Publishers http://www.influencepublishers.com.

ISBN: 978-1-645420-10-1 (Paperback)
ISBN: 978-1-645420-11-8 (eBook)

Published in accordance with the U.S. Copyright Office Orphan Works and Mass Digitization report of the register of copyrights, June 2015.

Originally published by Monarch Press.
Gregor Roy, 1965
2019 Edition published by Influence Publishers.

Interior design by Lapiz Digital Services. Cover Design by Thinkpen Designs.

Printed in the United States of America.

Library of Congress Cataloging-in-Publication Data forthcoming.
Names: Intelligent Education
Title: BRIGHT NOTES: The Rape of the Lock and Other Works
Subject: STU004000 STUDY AIDS / Book Notes

CONTENTS

1)	Introduction to Alexander Pope	1
2)	Introduction to The Rape of the Lock	18
3)	Brief Summary	39
4)	Textual Analysis	44
	Part 1	44
	Part 2	65
5)	Windsor Forest	86
6)	Pastorals	101
7)	Eloisa to Abelard	117
8)	Other Works	127
9)	Critical Commentary	134

10)	The Rape of The Lock: Essay Questions and Answers	141
11)	Other Works: Essay Questions and Answers	151
12)	Bibliography	154

INTRODUCTION TO ALEXANDER POPE

Alexander Pope, whose father was a linendraper, was born in London on the 21st of May, 1688. His parents were Roman Catholic, and Pope himself practiced his faith to the end of his life despite the bitter anti-Catholic sentiments of 18th Century England. The poet was further handicapped in life by the fact that he was crippled at the age of twelve by a disease which left him a hunchback less than five feet tall. Often the victim of contempt because of his religion and mockery due to his appearance, he gradually developed a bitter attitude toward life which reveals itself in some of his biting literary attacks on personal enemies. He never married, but was deeply attached throughout his life to a certain Martha Blount, and for a time to a Lady Mary Wortley Montagu, whom he later attacked bitterly in print. It is said that when he openly expressed his affection for her, she laughed at him on account of his deformity. Denied entrance of Oxford and Cambridge Universities because he was a Catholic, Pope was largely self-educated. Through his own labors he gained an appreciation of the classics, essential in the cultivated circles of the age, and a profound knowledge of the craft of writing. In Pope's age there were many strict rules which writers had to obey, and he mastered them more thoroughly and used them more skillfully than did any of his contemporaries. Principally due to his health and appearance, the events of his life are mainly literary ones, but he nevertheless led an active social life, and counted among his closest friends such eminent literary figures as the essayist Joseph Addison and the satirist Jonathan Swift. Yet he made more enemies than friends, and maintained fierce personal feuds which affected his writing and personality. His greatest and best known poem, *The Rape of the Lock*, was written when he was only twenty-four, and by his mid-thirties he was, rich and famous. He became financially independent due to his translations of Homer's *Iliad* and *Odyssey*, and this prevented his ever having to become a hack writer. His literary career can be divided into three periods, in which he wrote many types of poetry, from odes and pastorals to **satires** and philosophical poems. He died in 1744 and was buried at Twickenham, twelve miles from London.

HIS WRITINGS, FIRST PERIOD

The most important of Pope's early works are his *Pastorals*, which were published in Tonson's *Poetical Miscellanies* in 1709. Pope claimed that he wrote them when he was sixteen years of age, but this was never proved. It should be noted that Pope often made claims like this to make himself appear to have been an outstandingly precocious child. His *Essay on Criticism*, which was published in 1711, was his real introduction to the literary circle of which Joseph Addison was the center. In 1712, two works were published, one his Messiah, in the periodical, Spectator and *The Rape of the Lock*, in a publication called Lintot's *Miscellanies.* Of these two poems, the latter attracted immediate public attention and brought Pope a certain amount of acclaim. *The Rape of the Lock* was republished, with changes and additions, in 1714. In 1713 he produced a lyrical poem, his *Ode for Music on St. Cecilia's, Day*, but it was not a success. His *Windsor Forest*, however, which was also published in 1713, received a better reception, particularly in the political party known as the Tories. This reception was favorable because of references Pope made in the poem to the *Peace of Utrecht*. *Windsor Forest* is also important for starting the long friendship between Pope and Swift. As a result of his writings during these early years, Pope for a time became a member of Addison's group of friends, known as the "little senate". He soon broke away from it, however, to join what was called the "Scriblerus Club," a literary society which included such well-known contemporaries as Swift the satirist, and the poet John Gay. The two most important poems of this period, however, are his *Essay on Criticism* and *The Rape of the Lock*. At this point, a few general comments on these poems should be made:

1. *The Essay on Criticism* is the first poem of reasonable length that Pope published. It contains a remarkable number of lines which have passed into everyday speech as popular sayings. "For fools rush in where angels fear to tread," and "To err is human, to forgive divine" are two good examples of such well known quotations. It is wrong to regard this poem as a text of 18th Century critical opinion, however. Most of its contents are ideas borrowed from ancient writers, and were well known in Pope's time in any case. The poem's real value lies in its assertion that literary criticism is an art form which should be a living organism. And according to Pope, the critic will put life into his work by following "Nature" and her standards. We will shortly discuss what Pope meant by "Nature."

2. *The Rape of the Lock*, which we will examine in detail later, is a brilliant **satire** written in what is called a "mock-heroic" style reminiscent of classical **epic** poetry. A careful study of this poem not only gives the student a penetrating insight into the 18th Century method of

writing, but also offers a satirical view of the tastes, manners, and morals of the fashionable world in Queen Anne's reign. For poetical design and controlled proportions there was no contemporary poem to equal it. There is a dual satire in this poem, for Pope was ridiculing not only a trivial incident (the snipping of a girl's lock of hair) but also the high-flown style and language of **epic** poetry itself.

SECOND PERIOD

The middle period of Pope's creative life begins with the publication in 1715 of a translation of Homer's **epic** poem, the *Iliad*. This was only the first volume, however, the work being completed in 1720. By 1726 Pope had also completed a translation of Homer's *Odyssey*, and between them these two translations, made the poet rich, leaving him free to write what and when he wanted. In 1717 a collected edition of his works appeared, which is noted for the inclusion of two poems with love as their **theme**. This was unusual since, as we shall learn shortly, personal passions were not usually expressed in 18th Century poetry. In any case, these two poems were his Verses to the *Memory of an Unfortunate Lady* and *Eloisa to Abelard*. The first is an **elegy** to a lady who had committed suicide because of a hopeless love affair, and the second is a longer poem expressing the emotional anguish of a lady who is in love, but renounces love of man for love of God. During this second period, Pope made his one and only venture into the field of drama. In 1717 he helped the poet Gay to write a stage comedy called *Three Hours After Marriage*, but it was not a success. In 1723 Pope issued his **satire** on "Atticus," which was the name he gave to Joseph Addison, with whom he had quarreled. The fact that Addison had died in

1719 did not deter the poet from publishing his attack, which was rewritten and published again in 1735 under the title *An Epistle to Dr. Arbuthnot*. In 1725 Pope's edition of Shakespeare's works appeared. It contained several mistakes in scholarship which were exposed by a man called Lewis Theobald. This man was therefore picked by Pope as the main victim of a satirical work in three books called the *Dunciad*. The first version of this poem was published in 1728, bringing us to the beginning of his third period. The most important works of his second period, however, are his translations of Homer, and two points should be noted regarding them:

1. From a financial point of view, his versions of the *Iliad* and the *Odyssey* were a resounding success, earning him about (L) 9,000 (equivalent to about $100,000 today). This meant that Pope was now independent of publishers' demands and could spend the rest of his life comfortably in his country home at Twickenham. This triumph also meant that the poems had been most favorably received in literary circles. It must be remembered, however, that to meet 18th Century standards, a translation did not necessarily have to be accurate.

2. By classical **epic** standards, Pope's work on Homer is inaccurate and does not do justice to the originals. His translations are more faithful to the current poetic mannerisms of the 18th Century than to the **epic** grandeur of Homer. The Greek poet wrote in a very simple and direct manner, while Pope concentrated on producing elegant **epics** written in the polished style of the day. Where Homer says simply, "His father wept with him," Pope says that "The father poured a social flood."

THIRD PERIOD

The beginning of Pope's third and final creative period was marked, as we have seen, by the publication of the first version of the *Dunciad* in 1728. This was followed by three other editions in 1729, 1742 (called *The New Dunciad*), and 1743. In the completed Dunciad which had four volumes, the dramatist Colley Cibber replaced Theobald as the central figure being satirized. Between 1733 and 1734, Pope published "Four Epistles" of poetry, moral and philosophical in nature, which he called *An Essay on Man*. The poet added another epistle to this, and addressed it to Addison. During this last period, Pope published a collection of **satires** entitled Imitations of Horace, and the first of these appeared in 1733 under the title **Satire** I, which took the form of a dialogue. As was mentioned earlier, Pope and published his attack on "Atticus" (Addison) in 1723, which was later published in 1735, in this third period, as An *Epistle to Dr. Arbuthnot*. The reason for Pope's hatred for Addison, who had at one time been a friend of his, was the essayist's sponsorship of a translation of Homer to rival Pope's 1715 version of the *Iliad*. Although Addison died in 1719, Pope never forgave him, and continued the bitter attacks culminating in the 1735 poem. In the last years of his life, the poet occupied himself with the publication of his letters to his celebrated literary friends. Apparently in order to discredit a certain publisher called Curl, Pope employed very devious means of having his letters published by this man made public to make it appear as if this were done against the poet's wishes. He then produced revised versions of the same letters to make Curl seem dishonest. This indicates the bitterness which had increased in Pope over the years, and which stayed with him until his death in 1744. Of the poems in this last period, his *Essay on Man* and *Dunciad* are the most important and therefore worthy of some comment:

1. Pope had a twofold purpose in writing his *Essay on Man:* to justify God's ways to man, and to crystallize in poetic form some of the main ideas on man and society prevalent at that time. The poem contains such sayings as "The proper study of mankind is man," and "An honest man's the noblest work of God," both of which illustrate not only the thinking of the day, but also the concise way in which Pope expressed such thoughts. It must be remembered, however, that Pope was no profound thinker in a philosophical sense. In this poem he does not present any major system of thought or doctrine which is then developed and proved. It is, rather, a series of observations on man and the age, expressed in an urbane, clever way.

2. Pope wrote his *Dunciad*-or study of the dunces-as a major attack on everyone who had ever insulted him in any way. Much of it makes for rather wearisome reading, however, since many of the personalities upon whom he poured his scorn are totally unknown to us, as are the offenses which prompted the poet to launch his attacks in the first place. Nevertheless it does contain some brutally scathing comments on well-known literary figures-Daniel DeFoe, for example-which demonstrate the deep scars physical deformity and religious persecution had left on Pope's personality.

POPE'S OTHER WORKS

Apart from the works mentioned above, Pope's writings include his *Moral Essays* (1731-5), *Epistle to Augustus* (1737) and *Epilogue to the Satires* (1738).

THE 18TH CENTURY, SOCIAL BACKGROUND

Pope's position as a poet can be judged and appreciated to the full only when considered against the literary and historical setting in which he wrote. This period is often referred to as the Augustan Age, and the term could be used to embrace the years between 1660 and 1780 approximately, although for the sake of convenience we usually just say the "18th Century." It was an interesting century in English history, bracketed as it was between the rigid scholarship of the 17th Century and the scientific and religious skepticism of the 19th Century. In this age man showed a healthy, inquiring interest in the society around him, and was interested in the self as a part of the society. The Augustan Age is often criticized unfairly as being a period in which only decoration and flashy elegance were admired. In point of fact, society in all its different aspects, politician to servant, was examined and regarded by writers as their audience. And this society was not only studied and written about seriously, but also satirized quite ruthlessly, as we shall see in our study of Pope's poem *The Rape of the Lock*. If we look at some of the major works of English literature before this time-John Milton's *Paradise Lost* or Edmund Spenser's *Faerie Queene*, for example-we get the impression that writers wrote for a very limited public, unlike their Augustan counterparts. One bad feature of the age was the fact that a writer often had to depend on a private patron who would support him. The search for a patron could often be a degrading experience, and the great Dr. Samuel Johnson wrote a famous letter decrying patronage to Lord Chesterfield, who had humiliated him. Yet on the other hand, the patron's interests would often be expansive enough-ranging from politics to classical literature-to give the writer a wide scope of topics. Also, the printing press came of age in this century and received wide recognition with the publication of Pope's Iliad and Odyssey, which we have dealt with. This success also showed that writers could be independent of patrons. Commercially it was an age of expanding and healthy economy, when such institutions as the Bank of England and Lloyd's shipping agency were founded. London was the cultural and economic hub of England, and the center of its literary world. Civilized society in the Augustan Age meant in fact urban society which meant, in turn, London. Exotic things were admired-in *The Rape of the Lock*, for example, there is a reference to "all Arabia" coming from the heroine's perfume box - and there was a great interest in practical politics and in religion. The moral law, good sense and judgment, truth and superior taste were all held in high esteem. Homer was the favorite classical author, because he was sane and practical. It was an age of "neoclassicism," by which writers could analyze contemporary life in the light of the classics, but within strict literary boundaries, and of "humanism," by which man could fashion himself according to the best in past cultures. In this way man could learn to fulfill himself by learning how to live well.

LITERARY BACKGROUND

The basic rule by which Augustan literature operated was that man had to "follow Nature." By "Nature" was meant the pure standards of taste and judgment that should control all man's artistic endeavors. This demanded not only a knowledge of the classics and former civilizations, but also a strict adherence to set rules and regulations by which the artist would be guided in his representation of contemporary life. Everything had to be expressed with "wit," which did not imply "humor" as it does today, but meant rather the clear, clever expression of truth and reality. To achieve this clarity, ease and control, poets wrote a great deal in pairs of rhyming lines known as "heroic couplets," called so because they seemed most suitable for lofty **themes** which had to be expressed as neatly as possible. Pope himself was a master of this technique, and a good example of the heroic **couplet** - and of the Augustan philosophy - is his famous statement:

"Know then thyself, presume not God to scan; The proper study of Mankind is Man."

Art in Augustan terms had to be subservient to Nature - but according to Pope this meant what he called "Nature methodized." In this way, what often may appear artificial to us was "natural" to the Augustans. Outside the realm of literature, a good example of this process of "methodizing" and therefore improving Nature was the landscaping which Pope had done on his gardens at Twickenham. The result, artificial to modern eyes, was perfectly "natural" by 18th Century standards. The other names given to Nature were Reason and Common Sense, with which society had to be examined. This pointed the way to the writing of witty attacks on society, and the Augustan Age produced brilliant satirists, the most notable of whom were Jonathan Swift, who wrote *Gulliver's Travels* and *A Tale of a Tub* among others, and Alexander Pope. It was also an age of great essayists such as Joseph Addison and Richard Steele, whose prose contributions to the periodical journals *The Tatler* and *The Spectator* set a standard of style and tone in essays which is hard to equal. In fact, the rules of the age held fast for prose as well as poetry, and some writers-Swift and Addison-wrote both prose and poetry. There were, of course, some serious drawbacks in this attitude to art in general and poetry in particular. Too much stress on formalism tended to stifle the writer's freedom of expression, and an overdependence on the classics made the writing often stilted, "heavy" and Latinized. On the whole, the conformity of style led to monotony. On the other hand, there were some good points to counterbalance the bad. The demands made on writers led to a high degree of skill, discipline and clarity expressed in various art forms. These include the mock **epic**, the ode, the epistle and the epigram, types of poems which we shall discuss later. And of all 18th Century writers, Pope is undoubtedly the most skilled, polished and accomplished.

POPE AND THE 18TH CENTURY

In many ways Pope was very much the child of his age, its taste and its sensibility. When he wrote, he was often expressing not merely his own opinions, but those of his society. Now we spoke earlier about the 18th Century interest in man and society, and also said that earlier writers had a more restricted audience. While this is true, the Augustan view of culture was still limited by the rules which restricted the writers' style and sources. In this respect one wonders what would have happened to some of Shakespeare's great speeches had his language, style and sources been confined to strict areas. Pope therefore did not have the advantage of vernacular speech, for example, although he often used the conversational colloquialisms of his day to avoid becoming too academic. In keeping with his age, he always showed mature sophistication of outlook, never childlike innocence; poise and control, never recklessness and abandon; careful judgment, never passionate outpourings of emotion. He could nevertheless see through the shallowness of values which many of his contemporaries displayed, and was ruthless in his exposure of their flaws, as we shall discover when we study *The Rape of the Lock*. Above all, he took what his age offered him by way of literary standards and brought Augustan poetry to the pinnacle of technical artistry and skill. As spokesman of his age, he achieved the literary goal he himself set: to say "What oft was thought, but ne'er so well expressed."

POPE AND IMITATION

The Augustans used the word "imitation" to mean the re-creation of a work written by an earlier writer, but done according to 18th Century standards of style and formalism. Pope imitated many past writers-from Horace to John Dryden-for two reasons. First, he wished to maintain and be part of the great tradition of European literature; secondly, he took great pride in using an old expression, for example, and giving it a new turn of phrase and a contemporary meaning. Most of Pope's poems are in fact "imitations" and should be studied as such to obtain the full benefit of their contents. It should be made clear at this point that Pope did not just "repolish" old poems or phrases from poems, but rather translated the total effect of old poetry into polished Augustan phraseology. A good example of this is found even in certain passages of his early poems, the *Pastorals*, in which he successfully transfers the mood and tone of Virgil's pastoral Eclogues to the setting of an English countryside. His translation of Homer's *Iliad* and his poem *Eloisa to Abelard* are two of his better known works worth examing as "imitations." Pope's *Iliad* is not a good translation of Homer's **epic**, and he can be severely criticized-as he was by Samuel Coleridge, for example-for having really translated the 18th Century into ancient Greece. It is more successful if one forgets Homer and thinks of Pope drawing an Augustan picture using Homer's poem as his canvas. *Eloisa to Abelard* is an "imitation" of the type of epistle-or letter composed in poetic form-written by Ovid. This poem is also unsuccessful in one respect, inasmuch as the exposing of private passion and frustration, with which this poem deals, had no part in 18th Century literary expression. Through the brilliance of his capacity for "imitation," however, Pope nevertheless succeeds in capturing much of Ovid's vigor and intensity.

POPE AND SOCIETY

As we have seen, the Augustan Age was one in which urbanity of style, interest in man and society, and reverence for order-moral and otherwise-all found expression in its writings. While in one way it is true that Pope mirrored his society, in another sense he was uniquely separate from it. Being financially independent, he relied on no one for support; he moved in the highest social circles; and his literary position was established beyond question. All this allowed him to poke fun at, ridicule and attack-at times viciously - the aspects and members of society he found offensive. In *The Rape of the Lock*, for example, he makes a bitter comment about the contemporary legal system; on another occasion, speaking of the 18th Century in general, he said, "Not to be corrupted is the shame." On a more personal level, he bore deep grudges against people which he released in brilliant, biting and at times almost repulsive **satire**. The best example of this, of course, is his famous "war with the dunces," the *Dunciad*. Yet again we must consider Pope as a member of a literary society which, in the absence of libel laws, often reveled in personal defamation of character. Nor must we ever forget that Pope himself was throughout his life a very vulnerable target for other men's attacks, because of his deformity and religion, and there merely is something to be said for his personal bravery in so doing. For example, After the publication of *The Rape of the Lock*, Pope was actually threatened with physical violence by a certain Sir George Browne, whom the poet had caricatured in the poem as "Sir Plume. "Yet society to Pope was not there to be satirized, but also to be appreciated, and he often brought to his literary version of society what is too often forgotten about his poetry: a sense of enjoyment and fun, which will be appreciated in our study of *The Rape of the Lock*.

POPE AND THE CLASSICS

As we have already noted, a knowledge of the classics was essential to the Augustan idea of a civilized education. Homer was the ancient author most widely read, and it was not unnatural that Pope picked his *Iliad* and *Odyssey* to translate. But English writers in the 17th and 18th Centuries also turned for inspiration to French classicism, which had adapted traditional classical rules into its own code. Pope himself did not go often to French literary models for inspiration, but John Dryden did, and it was from Dryden that Pope received much of his taste for the classics. It is interesting that Pope was not influenced by writers like Spenser or Chaucer, whom he had read when he was young. In the true spirit of his age, he turned to more exotic sources such as Homer and Virgil, who was his favorite Latin writer.

Pope And Didactic Poetry

One of the main functions of the 18th Century poetry was that of teaching lessons to man and his society. This is known as **"didactic"** poetry. Pope again was a master of this art form, and the two poems which best illustrate this are his *Essay on Criticism* and *Essay on Man*. Although neither of these works sets out to prove one major issue, but flits more or less from one moral or critical saying to another, they are successful inasmuch as they impressed upon the reader's mind the particular point in question. Again, Pope in these poems is speaking not just on his own behalf, but for and to his age. Such lines as "Hope springs eternal in the human breast" and "A little learning is a dangerous thing" have passed into the language as everyday proverbs. It was not that Pope said much that was new-many of his thoughts are borrowed; but he said what was commonplace in a sparkling and unforgettable way. In a more negative way, even Pope's satirical poetry is **didactic**, for one of its purposes was to reveal the moral virtue of truth and honesty by exposing the opposite qualities in his victims. Hence we must bear in mind that his "Atticus" may not be a faithful portrayal of Joseph Addison; but at least "Atticus" lives for us as a type, and Pope is in fact telling us that the opposite type of person is much to be preferred.

POPE AND POETIC FORM

The type of poetic form which the Augustans found best suited to satisfy their demands for clarity and cleverness of expression was the heroic **couplet**. Pope achieved an unsurpassed degree of skill in the meter, rhyme scheme and technique of this form, although it took him a few years to master it completely. His creative process was to take a general idea, compress it into a precise thought, and then condense that thought into a heroic couplet with clarity and precision. In this way he may well have had an idea about Man and God when he started his *Essay on Man*; this was compressed into the thought that in his poem he (Pope) would be humorous where he had to be, that he would be honest, and that above all he would justify God's actions to mankind; and finally, when condensed into a heroic **couplet**, it came out in this way:

> Laugh where we must, be candid where we can; But vindicate the ways of God to Man.

From the technical point of view, Pope drilled his poems to perfection of meter and rhyme.

POPE'S STATURE AS A POET

During Pope's lifetime, there was very little doubt among his contemporaries that he was one of the greatest poets in English literature. Since his death in 1744, however, there has been a great deal of debunking of Pope as a poet. This criticism was particularly scathing in the 19th Century, when there was a general reaction against the tightly knit discipline of Augustan verse, and the clear, definite answers to the world's problems which Pope in particular provided in his polished way. He has been accused of a glossy shallowness of style and a restricted narrowness of vision, coupled with a refusal to "be himself" when he surrendered to the stiff, dogmatic rules of his age. His critics often point to the fact that his poetry lacks the unbridled passion which makes for great literature. It must be admitted that much of this criticism is valid. Pope's poetry and thinking was indeed limited by the rules and standards set down by his age. There is also the drawback to his poetry of the many contemporary references which make some of his writing almost unreadable. And it is true that the regular **rhyme** and rhythm of the heroic **couplet** make his poetry monotonous after a while. On the other hand, while it is true that he had no passionate interest in the "heroic" type of man depicted later by Lord Byron-who was, surprisingly, a great champion of Pope-or in "Nature" as a meant by William Wordsworth, Pope was nevertheless the outstandingly brilliant spokesman of his age. He analyzed, satirized, interpreted, praised and ridiculed the manners and morals of his day with devastating insight and incisiveness. As a master of satire and precise expression he stands unequalled and, while he admittedly adhered to the rhetorical cult of his age, it was, after all, his age. He was a victim of its faults and an exponent of its virtues. To the accusation that he was the polished master of "artificial" poetry, it could be argued that he was poet who most successfully mastered the artifice of polished expression. He has been chided for "preaching" too much in his poetry. We must not forget, however, that he was operating within the framework of the didactic school of literature which was part of 18th Century art. And, if we wish to see Pope at his most accomplished, a close study of his masterpiece. The Rape of the Lock, is almost essential. For it is in this poem that we can examine Pope the craftsman, satirist and scholar to best advantage.

GENERAL INTRODUCTION

Of Alexander Pope's poems, *The Essay on Criticism*, *The Rape of the Lock*, his translations of the *Iliad* and the *Odyssey*, the *Essay on Man* and the *Dunciad* are the most important and widely known. He wrote other poems, however, which are often neglected but are nevertheless worth studying to give us insight into his diversity and development as a poet. These minor poems, starting with the *Pastorals* in 1709 and ending with the *Universal Prayer* in 1738, span a creative lifetime in which Pope tackled a wide variety of poetry from lyrics and odes to **satires** and elegies. He was in his element with the brilliant type of **satire** so admired in the Augustan Age, and was not so comfortable with such forms as odes or lyrics, for example, where a more intense kind of personal emotion was demanded. We must take into consideration the restrictions of his age, however, as we examine the structure and content of his minor poems. Compared to other poets of his day, Pope shows in these poems the sensitivity and perception of a truly great artist.

INTRODUCTION TO THE RAPE OF THE LOCK

GENERAL BACKGROUND

Written when he was only twenty-four, this poem is Alexander Pope's masterpiece, and one of the finest examples of what is called "mock-heroic" poetry. One of its fascinating features is the fact that it is really a miniature **epic** poem, refashioning the classical features of poems like Virgil's *Aeneid* and Homer's *Iliad* and *Odyssey* to fit Augustan society. Pope hand three main aims when he wrote the work:

1. He wished to patch up a bitter public feud which had broken out between two well-known families. The incident over which the quarrel had broken out was a trivial one. The son of the one family had lightheartedly cut off a lock of hair belonging to the daughter of the other family.

2. There was a great deal of shallowness and useless frivolity in the upper-class society of Pope's day. Being a brilliantly perceptive man, he saw through much of this, and wished to ridicule it. When the opportunity arose to write this poem, he used it for this second purpose.

3. The Augustan Age was, as we have discussed, one in which classical literature-particularly Homer's **epic** poetry-was read widely. Despite the fact that Pope himself was to translate the Iliad and the Odyssey, he nonetheless found many of the time-honored **conventions** of the **epic** rather stilted and overdone. These **conventions** included the high-flown language, the noble descriptions of battles, and the intervention of the gods into human affairs To make fun of these **epic** features was his third purpose in writing *The Rape of the Lock*.

OBJECTIONS TO THE POEM

Some critics have objected that, while the poem is indeed attacking the shallow features of 18th Century society, it is itself a shallow work. These critics go on to say that the poem is nothing more than a practical joke set in fashionable terms. Pope has also been attacked for showing poor taste is having written the poem at all, and for displaying no moral values in it. These objections are easily answered:

1. Pope did not intend this to be a profound work-we have already seen his reasons for writing it.

2. Furthermore, considering the lack of tenderness in Augustan satirical writing, *The Rape of the Lock* is quite a gentle poem. Compared to Pope's own Dunciad, it is positively meek. We must never forget that Pope basically intended it as a piece of pure fun.

3. When we study the poem in detail, we will find that Clarissa's speech at the beginning of Canto V contains

all the high principles which Pope believed to be of more lasting value than those shown by the beaux and belles. This speech alone answers those who complain that the poem contains no moral principles.

HISTORICAL BACKGROUND

There were three prominent Roman Catholic families concerned in the incident leading to the poem's composition: the Carylls, the Fermors and the Petres. Pope knew the families' who all moved in the same social and literary circles as he did. The Fermors had a daughter, Arabella, and the Petres had a son, known as Lord Petre. Lord Petre cut off a lock of Arabella Fermor's hair as a joke, but the incident was not taken in jest, since a bitter quarrel ensued between the two families. The son of the Caryll family, John, asked Pope if he would write a poem to heal the breach. *The Rape of the Lock* is the result.

HISTORY OF THE TEXT

Pope himself said that the first draft of the poem was written in 1711, in less than two weeks' time. The poem was not published until 1712, however, when the completed work in two sections, called "cantos," appeared. This edition can in fact stand on its own merit as a polished and accomplished poem. Pope realized, however, that since one of his aims in writing the poem was to poke fun at **epic conventions** - often called epic "machinery" - he could not let the poem stand without making fun of the supernatural aspects of classical poetry. He therefore rewrote the poem adding tiny invisible spiritual creatures called "sylphs" which represent the gods of **epic** poetry. The final poem in five cantos was published in 1714, and this is the version which we read today. Some people have objected that the sylphs take up too much space, but this is a feeble argument against their presence. They blend beautifully into the structure of the poem, and add certain touches of whimsical humor and delight which in fact make their creation quite a stroke of genius.

THE POEM'S RECEPTION

By Pope's own account, Arabella Fermor was pleased with the poem when she first saw it, and was flattered at being its heroine. When the work was published in 1712, however, her attitude changed to one of hostility, as did that of the other principal characters in the poem. One of the victims of Pope's **satire** was a certain Sir George Browne-called "Sir Plume" in the poem who was so offended that he threatened the poet with physical violence. Pope answered the threat by writing that he wasn't worried, since a whipped wit is still as sweet as whipped cream. Apparently the hostility toward the poem on the part of the families concerned was of short duration. Apart from that, the poem was hailed generally as a masterpiece, and helped to make Pope famous. It was translated into French prose in 1728 and into Italian poetry in 1739. Accompanying both translations were descriptions of Pope as the greatest living English poet.

THE MOCK-HEROIC TRADITION

The Rape of the Lock belongs to the traditional type of poetry known as "mock-heroic." Pope himself described the work as an "heroi-comical" poem, and by this he meant the kind of poem that mimics the whole class of poetry known as "epic."

Epic poetry, considered the noblest type of literature, had always laid itself open to a certain amount of imitative ridicule because of its tendency toward overdone dignity bordering on pomposity. Mock-heroic treatment of some topic or other, however, does not imply that only classical poetry is being ridiculed. Contemporary society, with its shallow values and vanities, is under attack as well. It is to be noted that the moral content of epic poetry is never mocked; in fact, a poem like *The Rape of the Lock* could well be considered a moral work, since it advocates-mostly by implication - the values of truth, sincerity and decency. And it succeeds in its moral purpose by ridiculing the opposite values which were fashionable in the Augustan Age.

EARLIER MOCK-HEROIC LITERATURE

Western European literature had many models which Pope could fall back on for inspiration. In classical Greek literature, a mock-epic poem called *The Battle of the Frogs and Mice* was written in Homeric style, and is one of the best examples of this type of literature. It approaches its subject from two angles, treating insignificant subjects in a lofty manner, and reducing noble topics to ludicrous proportions. It should be noted that Homer was prone to introducing a mock-heroic tone even into his serious poems, by turning gods into men, for example. Later in history, the 16th Century Italian poet, Vida, wrote a mock **epic** called *A Game of Chess*, which Pope knew and used for some of his ideas. In 1622 another Italian poet called Tassoni published *The Rape of the Bucket*, in which the people of Bologna and Modena go to war over a stolen bucket. In one scene, an assembly of the gods is called for intervention purposes, but Juno cannot attend because of a hairdresser's appointment. This is the type of comic tone and situation Pope captures so effectively in his poem. But the poets from whom Pope received most inspiration for *The Rape of the Lock* were Boileau and Garth, whom we will discuss shortly.

SOME MOCK-HEROIC RULES

The Augustan Age was, we have seen, a time when poetic rules and regulations were treated almost with reverence. A famous 17th Century French critic called Le Bossu laid down certain rules for mock-heroic poetry, and these were followed to a certain extent by both Boileau and Pope. One of these was that mock-heroic poetry had to embrace as many **epic** qualities and **conventions** as possible. Pope does this by including in his poems such classical devices as **epic** similes-in Canto V, for example, he compares the confusion in Hampton Court to the earth-shattering events in Homer. As for battle scenes, the best example of a **simile** is, of course, the card game Ombre. The mock-heroic poem, according to Le Bossu, also had to be didactic and contain **epic** "machinery," such as gods. Pope's poem was **didactic** inasmuch as it set out to teach society a moral lesson by exposing insincerity and triviality to ridicule. The gods were introduced as sylphs. There also had to be a single action which takes place in the poet's own country. The action in Pope's poem takes place in London and concerns the events leading up to, including and following the removal of Belinda's lock. Pope goes even further than Le Bossu's rule for action by encompassing all the activities of his poem into half a day. But the two writers from whom Pope received the most ideas and with whom he can be compared to best advantage are the Frenchman, Boileau, and the Englishman, Garth, both poets of the Augustan Age.

BOILEAU'S INFLUENCE ON POPE

Boileau's famous poem was called *Le Lutrin*, and it was the first poem in modern literature to make fun of classical **epic** poetry by reducing features of great historical dimensions to absurd proportions. Yet far from mocking any moral which **epics** had to teach, Boileau's poem makes the moral impact of his poem stronger than that of classical **epic** poetry. This persuaded Pope to insert Clarissa's speech on values at the beginning of Canto V, and the inclusion of her address prompted the great Dr. Samuel Johnson to say that Pope's poem had a moral content deeper than Boileau's. Pope also borrowed from Boileau the idea of mock-epic speeches, divine agents appearing in dream form, and **epic** battles. Boileau took the opportunity to mock certain contemporary books by naming them during his "battle of the books." Pope copies him by making humorous reference to a book called Atlantis, which was popular in 18th Century fashionable circles. Pope was also strongly influenced by Boileau in his way of ridiculing and resolving **epic** battles. In the French poem, defeat in battle is prevented when the leader of those about to be vanquished raises his hand religiously to bless the apparent victors, who kneel down and are thus disarmed. The success of the absurd solution gave Pope the idea of including a similar scene in *The Rape of the Lock*. The result is the scene in which Belinda takes some snuff between her thumb and forefinger, and throws it in the lord's face.

GARTH'S INFLUENCE ON POPE

Garth, an English poet, published his poem, *The Dispensary*, in 1699 and made several changes in later editions, all of which Pope knew. The incident which inspired the work was an argument between the Company of Apothecaries and the College of Physicians over the distribution of free medicine to the poor. It is not a totally successful poem, however, lacking the control and power to make his **satire** effective. Pope was nevertheless indebted to Garth for two main improvements on *The Rape of the Lock:*

1. Pope got the idea from Garth of blending both serious and comic effects in one passage, sometimes even in one line. A good example of this is found in his description of Hampton Court, where he talks of the Queen taking counsel and tea-neither item funny in itself, but ludicrous in combination. This is a common type of figure in Garth's poem.

2. Perhaps the greatest influence Garth had on Pope was in his fondness for making satirical references to what was called the "beau monde" - the beautiful world - of Augustan society. One of the best examples of this in *The Rape of the Lock* is the magnificent but absurd description of Belinda's boudoir in Canto I. Here all the best features of mock-heroic poetry are found: the raising of trivialities to superhuman proportions, divine intervention in the form of sylphs, and the deification of an 18th Century belle.

CHARACTERS IN THE POEM

We must never forget that *The Rape of the Lock* is packed with contemporary references, and this includes well-known personalities. The Queen herself does not escape Pope's **satire**, nor do leading statesmen and aristocrats. On a more personal level, however, he made very pointed references throughout the poem to people directly concerned with the theft of the lock. Although he gave these personages fictitious names, this was a thin disguise which could not conceal their true identities from his contemporary readers. To the modern public, however, the names of these people, their family background, and their relationships with one another are meaningless. The following notes will provide the student with sufficient information about the characters in the poem:

Belinda

This was Arabella Fermor, daughter of Henry Fermor of Oxfordshire and Ellen Browne of Kent. The Fermors were a well-to-do Roman Catholic family who lived in the country but also owned a house in London. Sometime in 1714 or 1715 she married a Francis Perkins of Berkshire, and it is recorded that during her married life she and her husband entertained many leading Augustan literary figures including Pope himself. She died in 1737.

The Baron Or Lord

This was Robert, the seventh Lord Petre of Essex. In 1711-probably shortly after the cutting of Arabella's hair-he married Catherine Warmsley of Lancashire. He died in 1713 of smallpox, a reference to which is made at the beginning of Canto V. An interesting fact in English literary history is that the Petre family was also the subject of Edmund Spenser's marriage poem, Prothalamion.

The Muse

This was John Caryll of Sussex. Pope first met him in 1709, and their friendship, marked by a lengthy correspondence, continued until Caryll's death in 1736. It was he who persuaded Pope to undertake *The Rape of the Lock*.

Sir Plume

This was Sir George Browne, cousin of Arabella's mother. His caricature of "Sir Plume" is undoubtedly the most personally insulting in the whole poem.

Thalestris

Although there has been some dispute as to her identity, it is now almost certain that this was Lady Browne, wife of Sir George Browne. This makes the **satire** more biting, since Thalestris was an Amazon and Sir Plume was a fop.

Clarissa

Pope himself claimed that all the characters in his poem referred to people in real life, yet there is still dispute as to the true identity of Clarissa, who makes the speech at the beginning of Canto V. No conclusions have been reached, however, and her identity will probably remain a mystery.

It should be noted that the Carylls, the Petres, and the Fermors were all acquainted whether through friendship or marriage. John Caryll's letters, which are still preserved, show that all three families maintained a close relationship. One can imagine, therefore, how eager John Caryll was to patch up the quarrel between the Petres and the Fermors, particularly since it was over such a ridiculous incident.

PLACES IN THE POEM

Epic conventions, everyday incidents, and contemporary personalities were not the only objects of Pope's mock-heroic **satire**. Places were also ridiculed. Particularly in 18th Century London, being seen in the "right" places was every bit as important as wearing the "right" clothes or knowing the "right" gossip. Pope very cleverly brings some of these fashionable spots into his poem to heighten the humor. These few notes on what and where they were will give the student more insight into the **satire** of the poem:

The Mall

This was an enclosed walk which was built parallel to the front side of St. James' Palace. It was used initially as a court where pall-mall was played (pall-mall was a game similar to croquet). It eventually became a place where the beaux and belles came to stroll, gossip and, of course, ogle. It was not uncommon for musicians to play there, nor for dancing to take place there.

Hampton Court

The Hampton Court which Pope refers to was built by King William III, who often took up residence there. It is said that Queen Anne visited it infrequently. The Court faced onto oriental gardens, and this was the place where Augustan politicians and "wits" gathered to converse and make acquaintances. It is a perfect locale for the action of Pope's poem, although the real-life cutting of the lock almost certainly did not take place there.

The Ring

Next to walking in the Mall, the most popular form of relaxation for Augustan society was driving round the Ring, which was situated in Hyde Park. It was a kind of circular carriageway, where coaches used to drive, some one way and some the other, apparently in order that the occupants might see and be seen. It was large enough to take upward of 500 coaches at one time.

Rosamonda's Lake

This was a fashionable pond near the corner of St. James' Park. It was a popular meeting place where beaux and belles could exchange talk and glances.

All of the above named places were noted for elegance and style. Reference to them in a poem of this nature would naturally have more significance for Pope's contemporary audience than they do for us. Nevertheless, with a little bit of imagination, we can gather what they were like and the type of people who went to them.

THE USE OF SYLPHS

As we have already seen, there were two versions of *The Rape of the Lock*, one consisting of two cantos (334 lines) which was published in 1712, and the other consisting of five cantos (794 lines) which was published in 1714. The expansion of the second version was due to the inclusion of the sylphs, who come under the heading of what is called "**epic** machinery." In classical poetry, this machinery took the form of gods taken from ancient mythology, and they intervened regularly in the affairs of human beings. Pope borrowed this idea from the classics, together with three other ideas which can be briefly outlined:

1. The old idea that people on earth are guarded by the souls of their friends who have died.

2. The **convention** in classical **epics** whereby the heroes were assigned personal guardians from among the gods.

3. The idea of divine agents being regimented as in a regular army. In *The Rape of the Lock* Pope uses terms like "th' Aerial Guard" and "the lucid Squadrons" for comic effect.

Pope also borrows ideas from other poets in his use of sylphs. In the character of Ariel, for example, we can see elements of Shakespeare's Ariel from his play The Tempest. The sylphs too are sometimes reminiscent of the angels in Milton's **epic** poem, Paradise Lost.

THE GAME OF OMBRE

As we have already seen, one of the classical **conventions** which Pope set out to mimic in his poem was the **epic** battle. He did this by having three people, including the heroine Belinda, play the popular 18th Century card game known as Ombre. The green card table is described as a battlefield, and the cards as commanders and soldiers. We will not go into the intricate details of the game, but several points of interest concerning it should be noted:

1. It was played with forty cards, the value of each card depending on its color and on whether or not it was trumps. When a suit of cards, such as Spades, is made trumps, it means that any card in this suit can capture even the highest card in any other suit.

2. Each player was dealt nine cards in three batches, with three cards in each batch. The thirteen remaining cards became the "stock," and each deal started a new game.

3. When the players had the cards in their hands, they decided on who was to be the Ombre. The word Ombre comes from the Spanish hombre, meaning "man." The Ombre was the player who played independently against the other two, aiming to win by making more tricks than they. A trick is won when one of the players produces a card which is higher in value than the cards produced by all the other players. If the Ombre won the game, he or she was said to have got "Sacada," which means "something carried away." If either of the opponents won, however, he or she was said to have given "Codille" to the Ombre. In the poem we are told that Belinda barely escapes "the Jaws of Ruin, and Codille."

4. It is useful to remember that Pope was meticulously accurate in his description of the game in the poem. Belinda's way of playing Ombre has in fact been worked out on paper by card experts, and it is precise to the last detail.

5. When Pope talks of the "wily Arts" attempted by the Knave of Diamonds, he was drawing on the traditional idea that this was a card of ill omen.

STRUCTURE OF THE POEM

We have already seen how the final version of the poem consists of five cantos, or sections, totaling 794 lines. This is broken up into 148, 142, 178, 176 and 150 lines respectively per canto. It is written in regular rhyming couplets, and contains all the main features of Augustan poetry which we discussed in the general introduction. The changes in structure made in the 1714 version mainly affected the poem up to about the last 230 lines, which are almost the same as in the 1712 edition. The only major addition which Pope made to the 1714 version was Clarissa's speech in Canto V, which he wrote in 1717. The version we read today is nevertheless called the 1714 edition for the sake of convenience. Two comments should be noted with regard to these changes:

1. There has been some dispute as to the wisdom of Pope's having added Clarissa's speech in 1717 to a poem which seemed perfectly satisfactory in the 1714 version. Pope undoubtedly inserted the 26 lines to reinforce the moral message which, according to the rules, even a mock-epic poem had to contain. Those who find the speech offensive claim that the poem temporarily loses its tone of gentle ridicule when Clarissa begins to moralize. Those who defend its presence say that it adds the necessary serious touch which prevents the poem from becoming too frivolous.

2. The argument is often put forth that the 1714 version of the poem is uneven and out of proportion, compared to the 1712 version. It is claimed that the story of the poem is not a very expansive one, and that it does not warrant the extra 460 lines which made up the final edition. The counterargument to this is that the additions Pope made were necessary to fulfill all the functions of mock-heroic poetry. In this respect, it is essential for the student to remember that Pope was mimicking people, places, incidents, customs and **epics** themselves. Even 794 lines do not seem much for such a task, and the fact that he was brilliantly successful suggests that the additions were justified.

The Dedication

Pope wrote a prose dedication to Arabella Fermor which, although not actually part of the poem itself, is nevertheless interesting and worthy of a few comments. He begins modestly by saying that he wrote the poem merely to "divert a few young ladies," and to help them laugh at their own failings and those of others. Pope then apologizes to her for the incomplete 1712 edition, and goes on to explain the "**epic** machinery" of the sylphs in the later version. In doing so, he says that he bases the sylphs on the Rosicrucian doctrine of spirits, which he then proceeds to explain. The Rosicrucians, he tells her, believe that four types of spirit-sylphs, gnomes, nymphs and salamanders-inhabit the four elements, each of which represents various human conditions. He then very graciously assures her that the lock of hair is mentioned in the poem with reverence, and flatteringly tells her that the character Belinda resembles Arabella only in beauty. One cannot read the dedication without receiving the faint suggestion that Pope adopts a slightly "tongue-in-cheek" attitude even here.

GENERAL COMMENTS, BALANCE

It can safely be said, without any qualification, that *The Rape of the Lock* stands unequalled in English literature as an example of mockheroic poetry. Pope's blending of historical **epic** encounters-such as God versus the Devil or Greek versus Trojans-with trivial contemporary incidents and mannerisms, constitutes a masterpiece of imaginative ingenuity and technical skill. While everything is out of proportion in the poem in one sense-a card table becomes a battlefields for example-everything is beautifully proportionate in another sense. This proportion is probably best illustrated by the sylphs who, within the context of Augustan niceties, are perfectly credible and appropriate; even their names-Momentilla and Zephyretta, for example-are ideally diminished. Yet Pope never allows the mixture of social criticism and mock-epic grandeur to become stilted or rigid in any way; he never overdoes anything; his poem always maintains a mobility of style and a fluidity of content. It is a perfectly balance poem.

MACHINERY

We usually think of the sylphs when we talk of Pope's employing "epic machinery." The term "machinery" can also be used to embrace all the other aspects of classical **epics** which Pope sets out to mimic. The very fact that the heroine of the ancient Greek **epic** has been transformed into an 18th Century belle is itself absurdly effective. When the seizure of Helen of Troy becomes the stealing of a lock of hair, one begins to hear classical machinery creaking beside Pope's smoothflowing **satire**. Where Homer feeds his guests enormous beefsteaks in gigantic banquet halls, Pope pours fragrant coffee in fashionable Hampton Court - and Homer's feast seems somewhat ludicrous as a result. Achilles wields a gigantic shield in battle to protect his sacred body, while Belinda wears a shimmering petticoat in Hampton Court to guard her reputation - and Achilles' shield becomes absurd. That Pope was able to achieve this while sustaining his ridiculing of Augustan mannerisms shows his mastery over all the **conventions** of **epic** machinery.

VALUES

We spoke earlier of Pope's inserting Clarissa's speech in Canto V in order to reinforce the moral tone of the poem. Yet he also does this more indirectly throughout the poem by including subtle references to aspects of contemporary life which he found either ludicrous or repugnant. While he may refer to a tweezer-case in one part of the poem, we must not forget that he also scorns the politicians who sit drowsing in coffee houses. Nor should we neglect the bitter observation that at the very time Belinda and her opponents sit down to play cards, poor wretches are being sentenced to death in order that jurymen may have lunch. Although Pope was a Roman Catholic, he did not omit to insert a biting comment about too much concentration on dry works of medieval theology and Scholastic philosophy. In fact, nothing in society is too sacred for his **satire**, on condition that the object of his attack is something or someone estranged from the moral order which Pope himself revered. *The Rape of the Lock* could well be described as a poem of excellent taste, judgment and, above all, values.

CRAFTSMANSHIP

In this comparatively short poem, Pope took as much care with his craft as any classical **epic** poet ever did. He even went to the extent of playing solitary games of Ombre until he had worked out every moved Belinda and her opponents had to make to achieve his desired effect. His decision to introduce the sylphs into the 1714 edition, and the masterly way in which he lets them "melt" unobtrusively into the poem in itself proves Pope's dedication to the craft of poetry writing. From the point of view of meter and **rhyme** scheme alone, the poem is practically flawless. His **satire** too is always aimed at the appropriate targets: he knew classical **epics** well enough to see their ludicrous aspects; he was sufficiently well versed in the frivolous mannerisms and hypocrisies of his own day to mimic them with devastating effect. All this was accomplished with deceptive ease within the polished framework of the Augustan literary tradition, and is tribute to his painstaking work and craftsmanship.

WIT

As we learned in the general introduction, the Augustans did not mean "humor when they spoke of wit. They meant rather the cleverest and most skillful way of saying something-particularly something that had often been thought "but ne'er so well expressed," as Pope himself pointed out. But if, for our present purpose, we use the word "wit" in its modern sense as well, it can be stated quite definitely that this one quality which makes *The Rape of the Lock* an outstanding poem. From beginning to end it glitters with turns of phrase which crystallize as precisely as possible everyday ideas and observations. Pope's humor is often subtle and always sharp: his word portrait of the sylphs tugging at Belinda's earrings to warn her of impending disaster is typical of his highly imaginative sense of pure fun. It should be stressed again that the poem should be read primarily in this spirit of fun, for it was in this mood that it was written. All of this could well qualify Pope for the position of the perfect Augustan wit.

LANGUAGE

A study of *The Rape of the Lock* from the point of view of its language alone gives the student an excellent idea of what the Augustans meant by "correctness." Pope has a dread that the English language might have no future, and this was one of the first poems in which he set out to prove, syllable by syllable, that it did. For his linguistic model he turned, not to Greek, but to Latin, where he found that writers like Virgil and Ovid "packed" a line beautifully by sheer artistry of language. They also provided an element of surprise for the reader by the same method, and this was exactly what Pope was looking for in his poem. So when we read lines like "At length the Wits mount up, the Hairs subside," or "When Husbands or when Lap-dogs breathe their last," we find a synthesis of thought and expression inspired by Latin writers. The student will find that in this poem the sound fits the sense and the sense fits the sound with astonishing accuracy, due to Pope's superb use of language. An example is found in the line "Soft yielding minds to Water glide away."

EMOTION

We have seen how Pope's sense of fun runs through the entire poem. The student must not think, however, that Pope's emotions as shown in *The Rape of the Lock* are confined to clever witticisms. Admittedly, the Augustan Age did not stress the importance of displaying intense personal emotions in poetry.

Nevertheless, Pope does give rein in this poem to such feelings as righteous anger (in his comment about men being sentenced to death), contempt for sloth (in his remarks on politicians sleeping in coffee houses), and pity (in his indirect reference to Lord Petre's death from small-pox). On a more intimate note, Martha Blount-probably the only woman Pope ever loved-once said that Pope used to weep openly over passages of poetry he was reading. It should be pointed out, however, that these emotions displayed by Pope in *The Rape of the Lock* were by no means expressed in any outpouring of language. Again in the tradition of a Latin poet like Virgil, such expressions were always under strict control. Yet we must never think that Pope was devoid of emotion.

NATURE

In the general introduction we examined what the Augustans meant by the word "Nature," and here again a careful reading of the poem will give the student a firm grasp of all that it implied. By definition, Nature in the 18th Century sense stressed a general view of society rather than a particular one, and since *The Rape of the Lock* is filled with particulars, this poem would seem to be outside Augustan tradition. But what we really receive from this poem is general view of man in his 18th Century society through a detailed analysis of the particular aspects of man and society. The particulars of Belinda's boudoir, for example, or the description of the beaux and belles making their way up the river Thames by boat, give us an excellent over-all view of the upper-class mode of life in Pope's day. Reading this poem is like studying the Augustan Age through a microscope and still getting a superb picture of its literature, customs, delights, failings and institutions-everything the Augustans meant, in other words, by "Nature."

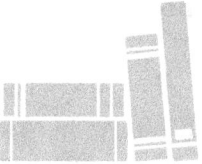

THE RAPE OF THE LOCK

BRIEF SUMMARY

CANTO I

The poem opens with an invocation to the Muse, John Caryll, and proceeds to outline the general **theme**, that of a terrible deed which had been done to a lady. The poet plunges immediately into the story by describing the details of Belinda's boudoir, and of the story heroine's gradual awakening. Ariel, her guardian sylph, addresses her in a dream in the form of a beau, and assures her that departed souls turn into sylphs who are invisible protectors of poor mortals. He warns her against the evils of vanity, but again informs her that the sylphs are always in attendance in case any harm should befall her-particularly at the hands of a scheming beau. Just then Belinda's lap dog, Shock, wakes her up by licking her face, and she proceeds with the rigors of dressing and making up for the day's social activities. Pope then proceeds to give a detailed account of Belinda's cosmetic preparation. He does this by describing her as a goddess and a priestess, performing sacred religious rites before an altar. The items of the "Toilette" are itemized for us like offerings to the gods. Gems from India, perfumes from Arabia, combs, pins, powder-puffs, Bibles and love letters are arrayed before her in all their magnificence. The harder Belinda works at her "Toilette" the more beautiful she becomes-her blushes become deeper and her eyes more sparkling. The canto ends with the sylphs fussing round the heroine like busy maids in attendance. Some fix her hair, others fold her sleeve, and some work on her gown. Belinda is now fully prepared for her emergence into the daylight, where she will face society looking radiantly beautiful.

CANTO II

We are now taken aboard a boat on the river Thames which will take Belinda, the beaux and the belles to the fashionable meeting place, Hampton Court. All eyes are upon the heroine, who smiles at everyone in order to offend no one. The two locks of hair that hang behind her are now described, and are compared to traps intended for man's capture. The scheming Baron sees the locks and determines that he will seize them by fair means or foul. In order to achieve his ambition, he builds an altar from French romances, garters and gloves; he then lights a fire with old love letters and prostrates himself in prayer. As the boat makes its way along the Thames, everyone is happy except Ariel, who, sensing disaster, calls all the spirits to a meeting. As they swoop down on the boat, their invisible wings give the impression of a breeze blowing. Ariel opens his wings and addresses them. He begins by outlining their respective duties: some spirits control the planets, while others pursue shooting stars; some cause storms at sea while others guard the British throne. Ariel and his spirits have the task of looking after the welfare of belles, however, and of maintaining their beauty. He tells them that some great calamity is about to take place, and that Belinda is to be the victim. The sylphs are therefore assigned various tasks: Zephyretta will guard the fan, Brillante the earrings; Momentilla will protect the watch, Crispissa the lock of hair; Ariel will guard

Shock; while fifty sylphs will watch over the petticoat. He ends his speech by outlining the drastic things that will befall any sylph who is neglectful of his duty. When he finishes, the spirits immediately proceed to their stations, where they await the terrible event.

CANTO III

We are now confronted with the boat's destination, Hampton Court. Pope describes it as the place where statesmen plot the downfall of nations overseas and maidens at home. Queen Anne sometimes takes advice here, and sometimes tea. The beaux and belles gather to gossip about topics ranging from the queen to furniture. It is now afternoon, and Belinda decides she wishes to play the card game Ombre against two noblemen. The cards are dealt, and various sylphs descend on Belinda's cards to defend them. The card game now commences, and is described as if it were a major battle. Four Kings, four Queens and four Knaves set forth to meet in combat. Belinda calls out that Spades are to be trumps. Belinda's cards go into action first, and she is victorious to begin with. Then the Baron attacks and he overwhelms the belle's cards by clever maneuvering; when his Knave of Diamonds captures her Queen of Hearts, she sees disaster ahead. But a quick turn of fate brings her victory. Coffee is then poured, and is described as if it were another religious ritual. The fumes attack the Baron's brain, and he decides to remove one of Belinda's locks. Taking a pair of scissors in his hand, he places them behind the lock, whereupon the sylphs spring to warn the belle, but in vain. The Baron snips her lock-cutting a sylph in two as he does so - and Belinda's screams of horror fill the air. The prize is won, and the Baron is full of glee, claiming that his name will be immortal because of this deed. The canto ends with a few lines on the power of steel; steel, Pope tells us, destroyed the labors of the gods when it destroyed Troy, and now it has ravished the hair of the unfortunate belle Belinda.

CANTO IV

The canto opens with a description of Belinda's almost unbearable anguish over the loss of her beloved lock. We are now introduced to the melancholy spirit Umbriel, who immediately goes underground to the cave of the goddess Spleen. She is in her dismal grotto with her handmaids Ill-nature and Affection. Foul vapors hang over the place, and objects like teapots and jars spring to life. Umbriel finds Spleen, and delivers a speech in which he tells her of Belinda's plight, and asks if the belle could possibly be affected with Chagrin. Spleen fills a bag with such strange items as sighs and sobs, then fills a vial with equally strange things like griefs and tears. Umbriel takes the bag and the vial back to earth, where he finds Belinda woebegone; he opens the bag above her head, and releases the furies. Belinda, suddenly enraged, bemoans her lost lock, but swears that she will get vengeance, and that the prize will not remain in the Baron's hands. She asks Sir Plume to recover her lock from the Baron; Sir Plume, a foppish fellow, makes a feeble protest to the Baron, which he ends by striking his snuff-box. The Baron shows contempt in his reply, and adds insult to injury by displaying the stolen lock on his finger. Umbriel then breaks the vial, releasing sorrows. Belinda becomes mournful, and gloomily broods over the terrible fate that has befallen her. She wishes that she had never seen Hampton Court, and that she could find some lonely isle to live on, where things like this can never happen. She then remembers the omens that had warned her earlier in the day, and that she had ignored. The lone lock hanging behind her remains as a permanent reminder of the calamity which has overcome her.

CANTO V

Everyone is deeply moved except the Baron, and now Clarissa starts to speak. She asks why it is that women of great beauty are always admired so much, when the virtue behind the beauty is what should be revered. She philosophizes that all the vain frivolities of the day do not succeed in banishing old age or curing small-pox, and that good humor and honor are far more powerful than empty beauty. She receives no applause. Instead, Thalestris calls for war, and immediately a furious battle ensues. Nothing Homer described equals this scene as beaux and belles enter the fray with gusto. Umbriel watches the battle, while some of the other spirits take part in it. Sir Plume is killed when Chloe frowns at him, but comes to life again when she smiles, Belinda takes some snuff between her thumb and forefinger, and throws it in the face of the Baron, who sneezes. The belle now removes a hairpin and threatens to use it as a dagger unless the lock is handed over. The Baron pleads for mercy, but Belinda insists, and her cries are louder than those of Othello in his anguish. Meanwhile, the lock has disappeared. Some people think it has gone to the moon, where very strange things are found, like broken vows and chains for yoking fleas. Suddenly, the Muse sees the lost lock, which has changed into a star, shooting through the skies followed by a trail of hair. The heavens glitter with the light it sheds, and the sylphs pursue it on its journey. Fashionable society will be able to see it forever from the Mall, and lovers will assume that it is Venus. Pope ends his poem by consoling Belinda: whens she and all her contemporaries are dead, the lock of hair which once adorned her beautiful head will shine on in the sky as a monument to Belinda's beauty. And her name will thereby be inscribed among the stars, renowned and immortal.

THE RAPE OF THE LOCK

TEXTUAL ANALYSIS

PART 1

CANTO I

Lines 1-12

The poem opens with a statement of how great injuries can be caused through reasons of love, and of the strife that can be created because of insignificant events. The poet invokes his Muse, Caryll, and introduces the heroine of the poem, Belinda. He asks what possible reason there could be for such a "gentle Belle" to reject a lord, for the lord's audacity, and for the lady's ensuing anger.

Comment

Pope is here using the traditional **epic** techniques of making a "proposition," or statement of contents, for the poem which follows, and an invocation to the Muse. He establishes the mock-heroic tone of the work immediately by making his Muse John Caryll, who had suggested that Pope write the poem to heal the breach between the two families. Lines 7 to 10 suggest vaguely that not all belles are necessarily gentle, nor all lords well-bred. His reference to "Little Men" in line 11 is an ironic comment on **epic** heroes, as well as on the fact that Lord Petre was a small man. Belinda is Arabella Fermor.

Lines 13-26

The story proper begins with the sun shining through white curtains, opening Belinda's eyes, which are brighter than the daylight itself. It is noon, the fashionable time for lap dogs and lovers to awake. To summon her servant, Belinda rings a handbell, knocks on the ground with her slipper, and presses her watch, which makes a "silver Sound." She falls asleep again, and her guardian Sylph summons a dream to come to her, in which he speaks to her in the shape of a handsome Beau.

Comment

Note how the mock classical formality of line 13 gives way to the 18th Century delicacy of line 18. The almost cynical coupling of lap dogs and lovers is tempered somewhat by the delicacy of the **couplet** itself. Lines 21 to 26 contain a good example of an **epic** technique used by Pope; that of contacting the hero during sleep. Here, of course, the **convention** has been placed in an 18th Century setting, although the absurdity is modified by a tone of gentle admiration for Belinda's serenity.

Lines 27-44

Ariel, disguised as a Beau, addresses Belinda as the ward of the Sylphs. He warns her that, if she has taken heed to her education by nurse and priest, she should be aware of her own worth and listen to advice from powers above mankind. She is assured of being well guarded by the invisible spirits of the lower sky, who are at all times hovering round such public places as the Ring.

Comment

The speech opens in the manner of **epic** delivery, and even the phrase "distinguish'd Care" is a direct translation from the Iliad. The nurse and the priest were considered in those days the chief sources of superstition, and the images in lines 33 and 34 are taken from hymns to the Virgin Mary. The Militia of the lower sky refers to aerial, rather than ethereal sylphs, and the Ring they protect was a circular carriageway in Hyde Park popular with fashionable society.

Lines 45-56

Ariel reminds Belinda that her guardian spirits, who act as her carriage, horses and footmen, were once beautiful earthbound creatures like herself, and had been transformed into sylphs when they died. He also stresses the fact that woman's vanity does not vanish after death, but continues to make her interested in such social niceties as guided carriages and Ombre, a popular card game.

Comment

Pope, in the deliberately high-flown style of the poem, is gradually setting the scene for the mock drama which is to ensue. The passing of souls from one body to another mentioned in these lines is called "metempsychosis." Pope got the idea from Ovid via the 17th Century poet Dryden. The reference to the card game Ombre is important, since the game plays a large part in the later development of the poem. It was played with forty cards, the value of the cards depending on their color and whether they were trumps.

Lines 57-66

The sylph proceeds to outline the various types of spirits into which the souls of the dead are transformed. This is determined by "their first Elements"; the spirits of fiery shrews become salamanders, for example, soft minds become nymphs, while prudish spirits remain earthbound as gnomes, prowling around in search of mischief. Flirts, on the other hand, become sylphs, flitting and capering through the air.

Comment

Pope is here drawing on the old idea that a person's character was formed according to the proportion of the elements in his body. He cleverly outlines the spirits in relation to their corresponding terrestrial elements: salamanders (fire), nymphs (water), gnomes (earth) and sylphs (air). He uses the word "fiery" in line 59 as a pun, referring to both the nature of the shrew and the element fire. The phrase "Fields of Air" in line 66 is taken directly from Virgil's Aeneid.

Lines 67-78

Ariel proceeds to assure Belinda that any belle who rejects mankind is automatically protected by a sylph, who has the ability to adopt any sex or form it wishes. He asks what it is that guards a maiden's purity from the treacherous designs of scheming males at balls and masquerades, when a girl is most vulnerable. Ariel answers his own question by telling her that the sylphs should get credit for what mortals normally call "honor."

Comment

Pope is making some references here to contemporary 18th Century society. "Midnight Masquerades," for example, were under attack at the time as being immoral assemblies, and the word "Spark" in line 73 was a contemptuous slang word for a showy type of man. Lines 77 and 78 are almost identical with a **couplet** from Dryden's Hind and the Panther, and is another example of Pope's willingness to borrow from earlier sources.

Lines 79-90

Belinda receives a warning that belles who are too vain come under the influence of the mischievous gnomes. These spirits work to inflate a maiden's pride, fill her mind with flirtatious thoughts, and at the appearance of nobility, redirect her innocence onto the downward path of the coquette. The sinister gnomes are, in short, forever plotting to besmirch a girl's virtue.

Comment

Pope maintains a tone of gentle **irony** in this passage, directed against the modish - and often hypocritical - attitude to female chastity which prevailed in 18th Century society. The phrase "sweeping Train" in line 84 is a cynical dig at the foppish dress of the aristocracy, and is taken straight from Dryden's *Aeneid*. The idea of the gnomes instructing belles in the art of flirting is borrowed from an article in the contemporary periodical *The Spectator* suggesting Ogling-Masters to train the young in the art of ogling.

Lines 91-104

Ariel reassures Belinda that when women are in danger of falling in this way, the sylphs are there to protect them. This they do almost cunningly, replacing one beau's advances with another's, insuring that the malice of one man's audacious advances is supplanted by another's gentle approach. Although mere mortals call this apparently fickle feminine behavior "levity," it is, in fact, divinely planned by the sylphs.

Comment

Again Pope continues his tongue-in-cheek commentary on the superficial flirtations, devoid of any emotional depths, which prevailed in his day; he attributes them to supernatural design rather than fashionable shallowness. The word "impertinence" in line 94 means "something trifling," and the reference to "the moving Toyshop of their Heart" comes from another Spectator article, in which the female heart is described as a toyshop. The "sword-knot" in line 101 was the ribbon made by a belle and tied round the hilt of her beau's sword. This whole passage is an example of Pope's mock-heroic treatment of the supernatural interventions of classical epics.

Lines 105-120

Ariel now introduces himself by name, and tells Belinda that he has descended from the air to protect her, since he received advance warning of some disaster about to befall her. He has no idea what the terrible event will be, but gives her dire warning to beware particularly of Man. Just then Shock, Belinda's lap dog, wakes her with his tongue, and she opens her eyes. The first thing she sees is a love letter, but the vision in her dream has vanished.

Comment

This passage contains several samples of Pope's habit of borrowing ideas and devices from other poets. The "Protection" technique in line 105, for example, comes from the Iliad, while line 105 is a direct copy from Dryden's way of starting a narrative poem. The remainder of Ariel's speech, from line 107 to 114, is reminiscent of Uriel and Gabriel's speeches in Milton's *Paradise Lost*. The "clear Mirror" and "ruling star" in line 108 are images used together in Plato's *Timaeus*. The warning technique between line 112 and 114 was used often in classical epics, e.g., Hector's ghost warning Aeneas to flee on the night Troy was sacked in Virgil's *Aeneid*. The name "Shock," given to Belinda's lap dog, comes from the "shough," a species of Icelandic dog imported into England at this time.

Lines 121-132

This begins the description of Belinda's boudoir and her preparations for the day's activities. Amidst silver vases-containing, presumably, cosmetics-Belinda admires herself in the mirror. Her image is described as a goddess, she herself as a priestess, and her furniture as an altar. She proceeds to lay out the clothes and accessories with which she is going to adorn herself.

Comment

Pope describes the ritual of Belinda's "Toilette" with **epic** solemnity. The vases in her boudoir are arranged to suggest mystical rites reminiscent of the ancient classics, and this is reinforced by the **allusion** to Belinda's image as a goddess and to herself as a priestess making offerings on an altar of furniture. The mock-heroic tone is sustained with superb control throughout this whole passage, to the end of the canto.

Lines 133-148

There now follows a detailed description of the contents of Belinda's boudoir. Gems from India, perfumes from Arabia, and combs made of tortoise shell and ivory are arrayed, as well as "Puffs, Powders, Patches, Bibles, Billetdoux" - a line often quoted from the poem. Belinda proceeds to adorn herself and apply the cosmetics which will heighten her natural beauty, making her blushes more pure and her eyes more sparkling. The canto ends with the sylphs fussing round Belinda, acting as hairdressers and handmaids.

Comment

The references here to India and Arabia are examples of Pope's occasional comments in the poem to places and events outside the rarified atmosphere of upper-class London society. The famous line 138, quoted above, is in fact a **parody** of the line "Rocks, Caves, Lakes, Fens, Bogs, Dens, and shades of death" from Milton's *Paradise Lost*. In line 139, Pope is parodying the preparation of the **epic** hero for war, and it could well have been copied from Dryden's line, "I see fair Helen put on all her Charms." The last line of the canto is a direct reference to the Iliad, and the "Betty" in this line is in fact Belinda. Pope borrowed the names Betty and Belinda from Congreve's play *Old Bachelor*.

CANTO II

Lines 1-18

Belinda sets forth upon a trip on the Thames to Hampton Court. She is compared to a sunbeam because of her radiant beauty, and all eyes are upon her. Around her neck she wears a cross, her mind is lively and her looks are alert. She grants everyone the favor of her smiles, and, if she has faults, they are certainly well concealed beneath her sweet exterior. In any case, one glance at her beauty would make you forget any blemishes in her character.

Comment

In his use of exaggeration, Pope is poking gentle fun at Belinda, who is described in the same way goddesses were described in ancient epics. Belinda's trip on the Thames is reminiscent of

Aeneas' voyage on the river Tiber as outlined in Virgil's *Aeneid*. The word "ease" in line 15 is used in the 18th Century sense of a quality arising from good breeding.

Lines 19-28

We are now introduced to the two locks of hair that adorned Belinda's neck. They spell doom to mankind, and are compared to bird traps and fishing lines created to lure and ensnare some unfortunate male.

Comment

Pope really becomes expansive here in his mock-epic description of the two locks and their supernatural powers of destruction. The poet is here using a traditional Greek image borrowed by English writers. Dryden brought this idea into some of his poetry, and Milton referred to women's hair as a net for trapping men.

Lines 29-46

The lord-called here the "Baron" - now makes his appearance. He sees the locks, and immediately lays plans to obtain them by fair means of foul. We are told that when a lover wants his way, few inquire as to his method of attack. The lord now builds an altar to the Goddess of Love, composed of twelve French romances, three garters, and a glove, all of which are relics of his past love affairs. He lights a fire to the Goddess with love letters, and fans the flames with sighs of love. He throws himself down in front of the altar and prays that he might win the hair and keep it. Half of his prayer is granted, while the wind blows the other half away.

Comment

The traditional **epic** hero is being satirized here with devastating **irony**. Praying to the gods before entering battle was, of course, a traditional ancient ritual, and in this passage both the hero and the tradition are mocked by making them appear ludicrous. The antithesis "By Force . . . or by Fraud" in line 32 is a popular one in **epic** poetry. The lord's altar-building described between lines 36 and 42 is almost identical to an incident in Chaucer's *Knight's Tale*, and the reference to the wind blowing half the prayer away comes from Virgil's *Aeneid*.

Lines 47-58

The boat taking Belinda, together with other belles and beaux, to Hampton Court, makes its way over the waves to the sound of music. Belinda smiles, and the whole world brightens except Ariel, the sylph, who broods over the forthcoming tragedy. He calls a meeting of all the sylphs, who descend upon the ship immediately. Their fluttering whispers are taken by the passengers to be gentle winds.

Comment

Pope is again employing the classical device of the gods directing the destiny of mortals. The image of Ariel, the sylph, brooding alone and unseen amidst the happy throng is again a ludicrous one in keeping with the general spirit of the poem. The "floating

Tydes" of line 48 is taken straight from Dryden, and the word "Denizens" in line 55 is used to mean "foreigners who have become citizens." The idea of regimenting the spirits in line 56 was a popular one in Pope's day.

Lines 59-72

The sylphs are described here in detail. They are too transparent to be seen by mortal eyes. They flit around in the breeze, some unfolding their wings in the sunlight, others floating freely in the bright light, their wings changing colors to match the skies. Ariel, who is slightly larger than the rest, sits on the boat's mast, unfurls his wings, raises his wand to get attention, and addresses the gathering of sylphs.

Comment

The **allusion** to "filmy Dew" in line 64 comes from the old myth that gossamer, which the sylphs resemble, was made from dew. The changing colors of the sylphs to match the skies is reminiscent of a reference to "colours dipt in Heav'n" which Milton makes in *Paradise Lost*. By making Ariel taller than the rest, Pope is sticking to the **epic** tradition that the hero was always taller than his followers. Ariel's wand in line 72 is colored blue to blend with the sky.

Lines 73-90

Ariel begins his speech to the sylphs, to their female counterparts, the sylphids, and to the other species of spirits, by outlining their respective duties. Some flit around the air, others bask in the sun; some guide the planets, others have the less dignified job of following shooting stars; some inhale the mists of the lower atmosphere, while others dip their wings in the rainbow; some cause storms to rage on the sea, and others cause the gentle rain to fall; some guide and guard the ways of men; of these the most elite are chosen to protect the British throne.

Comment

Again Pope is using a classical **epic** concept here in a gently ironic way. The cataloguing of the different occupations of divine creatures was a traditional part of **epic** poetry, and is found in such works as Virgil's *Aeneid* and Milton's *Paradise Lost*. Line 80 is copied from the *Iliad*. The reference to British royalty in line 90 shows that no level of society escaped Pope's satire.

Lines 91-100

The chief sylph proceeds to outline for the assembled spirits the task at hand, namely the guarding and care of the belles. Their duties will include preventing the wind from blowing away their face powder; stealing colors from rainbows to be used as tints; curling hair and improving blushes; or instructing the belles, through dreams, to alter the frills on their petticoats.

Comment

Pope is poking fun at feminine vanity in this passage. The absurdity of the switched roles of gods to sylphs and Greek heroes to 18th Century belles becomes increasingly pronounced with every detail Pope outlines—shields and armor being transformed to petticoats, for example.

Lines 101-116

Ariel now warns them of the impending disaster which lies in wait for the fairest belle of all, Belinda. The Fates have kept the details a secret, however, so he proceeds to outline some of the disasters that could possibly overtake her. Belinda may tarnish her honor or break a China jar; perhaps she will forget to pray or to attend a masquerade; at a ball she may lose her heart or, worse, her necklace; she may even lose her lap dog, Shock. He then assigns special tasks to individual sylphs, naming each one as he does so: Zephyretta guards the fan; Brillante the earrings; Momentilla the watch; Crispissa the favorite lock of hair; while Ariel himself has the honor of guarding Shock.

Comment

The warning of forthcoming disaster occurs time and time again in classical epics, and Pope uses it here in true mock-heroic fashion. His irony is in full swing when he lists the possible disasters that could befall Belinda, making a trivial event, like staining brocade, for example, more important than staining honor. The names Pope gives the sylphs are delightfully appropriate to the fragile portrait he has drawn of them.

Lines 117-136

Fifty specially selected sylphs are given the job of tending Belinda's petticoat, which requires such a large number because of its width and awkwardness. Ariel then ends his speech by issuing a dire warning to spirits who in any way neglect their duties. Some will be bottled up and others transfixed with pins; some cast into a bitter lake, others stuck in the eye of a needle; some shall have their wings glued with gum, while others will be shriveled up; some shall suffer Ixion's fate on a wheel, and the remainder will choke in fumes of burning chocolate over a foaming sea.

Comment

Pope is making direct reference here to the **epic** shield as used in the Iliad, the shield becoming, in this case, a petticoat. The punishments to be meted out to wayward sylphs are an incongruous **parody** of the penances given to souls in Hades as outlined in Virgil's *Aeneid*. The word "Bodkin" as used in line 128 is a needle with a blunt point; elsewhere in the poem it has other meanings. Ixion was a king in Greek mythology whom the gods punished by strapping him to an eternally rotating wheel.

Lines 137-142

At the end of Ariel's speech, the sylphs come down from their perches on the boat's sails, some to guard Belinda's hair and others her earrings. The canto ends on a note of tension, with the spirits breathlessly awaiting the dire event.

Comment

The end of the canto leaves the reader in suspense, again with mock solemnity and classical style. The description of the sylphs descending on Belinda "Orb in Orb" in line 138 is a **parody** of the angels in *Paradise Lost*. The last line, in which the **catastrophe** is anticipated, is an imitation of a line in the *Iliad*.

CANTO III

Lines 1-8

The canto opens with a description of the majestic towers of Hampton Court, the destination of the boat carrying Belinda, the beaux, the belles, and the sylphs. It is here, Pope tells us, that Britain's statesmen plan the downfall of foreign tyrants, and Queen Anne takes advice - and tea.

Comment

Pope directs his **satire** here against contemporary British royalty and aristocracy. There is more than a touch of **irony** in his referring to the victims of British imperialism as "tyrants" and in this making Queen Anne take advice and tea in the same line. This figure of speech, in which a single verb-in this case "take" - has as its objects two incongruous words for comic effect-in this case "Counsel" and "tea" - is called zeugma. The "three Realms" are England, Wales and Scotland.

Lines 9-18

The beaux and belles, whom Pope calls "the Heroes and the Nymphs," arrive at Hampton Court and indulge in discussing various topics of great interest: who gave a ball or paid a visit to whom; the glory of royalty or the charm of an Indian screen; the meaning of glances. Characters are torn to shreds, and conversation is interspersed with the taking of snuff, the fluttering of fans, laughter and, of course, ogling.

Comment

This is a delightful comment on the shallowness and frivolity of contemporary society, written in a gently ironical tone. Indian screens had become very fashionable in 18th Century England, and the taking of snuff became popular in Queen Anne's reign.

Lines 19-36

It is now afternoon, the time of day when judges and juries get hungry and sentence men to death so that they may eat. The labors of the "Toilette" are over, and Belinda wishes to play Ombre, and card game, with two knights. The cards are dealt, and the sylphs descend immediately upon Belinda's important cards: Ariel sits upon a Matador, and the other sylphs sit on cards in order of their importance. Pope informs us that sylphs, like women, are fond of social position.

Comment

Pope draws on many classical **epic conventions** in this passage, which leads into the description of the card game seen as a major battle. Lines 21 and 22, referring to the death sentence, contain a scathing comment on the callousness of the contemporary judiciary system. From line 29 on, Pope puts his mock-heroic techniques to full use, starting off with the sylphs sitting on the cards in order of rank, just as the gods in Virgil's *Aeneid* were placed according to their station.

THE RAPE OF THE LOCK AND OTHER WORKS

Lines 37-46

The cards are described here. First, there are four Kings with white whiskers and forked beards; next, four beautiful Queens, each with a flower in her hand; then there are four Knaves with hats on their heads and battle axes in their hands; and finally there is an array of multi-colored soldiers ready to do battle upon the velvet card table. Belinda examines her cards carefully, and calls for Spades as trumps.

Comment

This is a military review in the true **epic** tradition, as in the *Iliad*, for example, with the leaders and troops primed for battle. It should be noted that Pope was meticulously accurate in his details of the card game, and his whole description of the battle of the cards is a brilliant example of epic devices being employed with tongue-in-cheek dignity. Belinda's exclamation on trumps in line 46 is a direct reference to the "Let there be light" of the Bible - an example of Pope's using the sublime in a ridiculous setting.

Lines 47-64

Belinda's Matadores move into battle first, like Moorish warriors. Spadillio, an unbeatable commander, captures two trumps and sweeps the whole board. Manillio also attacks successfully, and marches triumphantly from the green battlefield. Basto is less successful, capturing only one trump and one plebeian card. The King of Spades makes his appearance and displays one of his legs, the rest of his body being concealed beneath his rich cloak. The rebellious Knave, who dares tackle his own King, is justly defeated. Pan, who has been so victorious in the past, is now without assistance and is well beaten by the King of Spades.

Comment

Pope is here making fun not only of the solemn in way which Ombre was played in his day, but also of the whole tradition of **epic** battles. He uses the names of the cards, like Manillio and Basto, in the same way the names of junior commanders are used in classical epics. The Moors in line 48 are referred to in the same way as the African warriors in Virgil's *Aeneid* are mentioned. In line 64, Pope is borrowing directly from the *Iliad*.

Lines 65-86

So far Belinda has beaten both opposing armies. Now fate decrees that the Baron takes the field, and his Amazon attacks the King of Spades' troops. Next, his Diamonds attack, and the colorful King who shows only half his face, together with his shining Queen, are easily triumphant over the broken line of troops. Clubs, Diamonds, and Hearts lie scattered about the green, and the battalions of African and Asian troops fall in heaps, destroyed by fate.

Comment

The card game is now described as a battle in full swing. Even adjectives such as "Embroider'd" and "refulgent" in lines 76 and 77 are found often in descriptions of clothes in the Iliad. The description of the army being routed between lines 81 and 86 is a **parody** of Hannibal's defeat by Scipio in North Africa.

Lines 87-100

The crafty Knave of Diamonds now captures the Queen of Hearts. Belinda turns pale at this, and foresees the ruin that is going to befall her. One trick would bring her victory. The Ace of Hearts shows himself, and Belinda's King, who has been lurking in her hand to avenge the capture of his Queen, pounces on the Ace. Belinda whoops with delight, and the walls, woods and canals answer her.

Comment

Note the clever way Pope uses economy of description in this passage to heighten the excitement. Nothing is overdone, and the atmosphere of a battle is maintained as well as the **irony**. The word "trick" in line 94 is used in two senses. The King's leap upon the Ace in lines 98 and 99 is reminiscent of the victor pouncing upon the prize in the *Iliad*.

Lines 101-104

This is a lamentation on the fact that mortals are blind to fate. They are dejected easily, and rejoice just as easily. We are warned that the spoils of the victory which Belinda has just won will soon be removed from her.

Comment

Again in true **epic** tradition, Pope here interjects a dire warning to mortals who pay no heed to fate. There is a similar passage in Virgil's *Aeneid*, and the phrase "blind to Fate" in line 101 is found in the *Iliad* and the *Odyssey*.

Lines 105-124

Cups and spoons are placed on the card table in preparation for coffee, which is then ground down. A lamp is raised onto a lacquered table, the coffee is made, and then it is poured into China cups. The group proceeds to drink many cups, while the sylphs descend on Belinda: some blow on her coffee, while others spread their wings to protect her brocade. Meanwhile, the fumes from the coffee attack the Baron's brain, and make him plot the cutting of Belinda's hair - the rape of the lock. Pope warns the lord of the punishment which Fate imposed on Scylla, who was changed into a bird for plucking out Nisus' hair.

Comment

Pope is here concentrating his satirical powers not so much on 18th Century society as on the great feasts described in **epic** poetry. If we bear this in mind, the ritual of pouring coffee takes on ludicrous dimensions. The "shining Altars of Japan" in line 107 is a high-flown way of describing the process of varnishing tables known as "japanning." The sylphs are described between lines 113 and 116. The reference to the coffee fumes filling the lord's brain with plots is a comment on the coffeehouses of the day, where politicians met to plan their policies. The story of Scylla stealing the magic strand of purple hair from King Nisus' head to give to her beloved Minos, and being changed into a bird for her impiety, is told by both Ovid and Virgil.

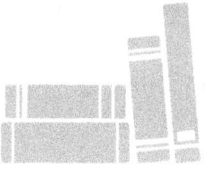

THE RAPE OF THE LOCK

TEXTUAL ANALYSIS

PART 2

Lines 125-138

A new character appears-Clarissa, who removes a pair of scissors from her case and presents it to the lord in the same way as ladies in romances arm their knights. He takes them and, as Belinda bends over the steaming coffee, he stretches out his hand behind Belinda's neck in preparation for the attack. Immediately a thousand sylphs rush to warn her, furiously beating their wings. Three times they twitch the diamond in her ear; three times Belinda turns her head; and three times the enemy scissors approach her neck.

Comment

Pope describes the scene as a preparation for the kind of battle assault common in classical epics. The "Engine" in line 132 is a reference to any large military machine - in this case the scissors - and the number of sylphs (a thousand) is a popular one in epics.

Lines 139-146

Ariel now makes a desperate attempt to reach Belinda's mind as he sits upon her nosegay gazing at her thoughts. He suddenly sees that she has a beau on her mind, and, finding himself at a loss, retires with a sigh of despair.

Comment

This is a delightful **parody** of the whole concept of the Guardian Angel, made more absurd by Ariel's perch on Belinda's flowers. The fact that the only thing Belinda can think about is her beau makes her goddess-like portrayal even more ridiculous.

Lines 147-160

The lord now closes the menacing scissors to snip the lock from Belinda's neck. As he does so, an unfortunate sylph gets in the way and gets cut in half. Sylphs have magical powers of recuperation from such disasters, however, and the two parts join up again. The scissors close, and the lock is severed from her hair forever. Lightning flashes from Belinda's eyes, and screams of horror rend the air. No greater commotion is caused when husbands or lap dogs die, or when China cups are accidently broken.

> Comment

The sylph's getting caught by the scissors is Pope's way of parodying the angel who interposes when Saul flings the spear at David. The phrase "fatal Engine" in line 149 is also used by Dryden in his Aeneid, referring to the wooden horse outside Troy. The comparison between the **catastrophe** being described and other similar calamities is a common one in **epic** poems - the *Iliad*, for example. In this instance the comparison of the lock with husbands and dogs intensifies the absurdity.

Lines 161-170

The lord calls for a laurel wreath to celebrate his triumph. He announces that his fame will live as long as fish find pleasure in water, birds delight in air, the British ride in "Coach and Six," the Atlantis is read, small pillows are found on ladies' beds, visits are paid by candlelight, and belles receive favors from or have rendezvous with their beaux.

> Comment

The wildly exaggerated extension of the lord's victory is an old tradition in **epic** poetry, and Pope is using it here to ridicule both its use in poetry and the shallowness of some contemporary social customs. The Atlantis was a popular libelous work by a Mrs. Manley, and the visits referred to in line 167 were 18th Century social rituals in which ladies visited one another accompanied by servants carrying candles.

Lines 171-178

Pope ends the Canto by paying tribute to the power of steel. Both monuments and men fall under steel; steel destroyed Troy and has caused the destruction of triumphal arches. How then, the poet asks, could Belinda hope to avoid **catastrophe** because of steel?

Comment

Pope ends this part of the poem with a rhetorical question, which is a question to which the answer is obvious. This is another classical epic device, and the poet brings it in here to round off the canto in the mock-heroic vein that runs through the whole poem.

CANTO IV

Lines 1-10

Belinda is overcome with anguish and anger due to the loss of her beloved lock. No one has ever experienced such grief and rage: kings captured in war, disdainful virgins who survive their charm, passionate lovers deprived of joy, old ladies whom no one will kiss, tyrants who die unrepentant, Cynthia when her mantua is askew - none has ever known such despair.

Comment

The **irony** of this passage lies not only in the exaggerated degree of Belinda's grief, but also in the incongruous coupling of such examples as captive kings and frustrated old maids. A mantua was a loose upper garment worn by 18th Century ladies.

Lines 11-24

We are now introduced to Umbriel, a gloomy spirit who makes his way to the underworld to find the Cave of Spleen. He flaps his black wings through the mists of the cave, where only the chill east wind blows, and there, in a grotto sheltered from clean air and light, lies Spleen, the goddess of the underworld. Two attendants are by her couch. Their names are Pain and Megrim.

Comment

In classical epics, journeys to the underworld are frequently outlined, as in Ovid's *Metamorphosis*, for example, where a dungeon is described in a way which suggests that Pope used it as his source for the Cave of Spleen. The name of Pope's goddess, Spleen, is in fact the illness of jealousy which was reputed to be suffered only by the idle rich. The east wind is used in line 20 because, according to tradition, it helped to promote spleen. Pain and Megrim are allegorical figures, of course, and Pope is here poking fun at this time-honored **epic** device. Megrim is migraine, or a severe headache.

Lines 25-38

Two handmaids wait on Spleen. One is Ill-nature, an old hag dressed in black and white, with prayers in her hands and lampoon in her bosom. The other is Affectation, a sickly young woman who has practiced all the feminine arts like lisping and languishing. Belles of the day, we are told, become ill in this way every time they wear a new night-dress.

Comment

The black and white dress is a reference to the traditional idea that ill nature puts the human race into two sections. One is white (for virtue) and it is empty. The other is black (for vice) and it is full. In Pope's day there were bitter attacks, particularly in the periodicals *Spectator and Tatler*, against affectations like lisping, which was becoming a fashion among men. The poet is here adding his scornful protest.

Lines 39-54

A mist hovers over Spleen's palace, and ghosts arise as fearsomely as the dreams of hermits and as vividly as the visions of dying belles. Fiends, snakes on spires, tombs and fires appear, together with lakes of gold, heavenly domes, and angels in machines. Many bodies take the change shape under Spleen's direction: teapots spring to life, pipkins start walking like Homer's Tripod, a jar sighs, a goose-pie starts talking and belles who have turned into bottles start shouting for corks.

Comment

This passage begins with a reference to the hallucinations that victims of the spleen were said to have. Pope then pokes fun at religious enthusiasts-particularly belles-who have "visions." The poet, himself a Roman Catholic, often expressed suspicion at such claims. The description of the creatures and features of the cave catalogued between lines 43 and 46 is Pope's way of mocking some of the ludicrous scenes in contemporary operas. The change of shapes from line 47 to line 54 also refers to the kind of hallucinations experienced by spleen victims. A pipkin was a small three-legged earthenware vessel for boiling water.

Lines 55-78

Umbriel, carrying a branch of "Spleenwort," files through this strange scene and addresses Spleen. He praises her for her command of belles from fifteen to fifty, for inducing hysteria and poetic inspiration, for making people take medicine and write plays, for making proud people postpone visits, and for sending the pouting devout to prayer. He tells her that Belinda scorns Spleen's powers, and that just as he can make pimples rise on belle's cheek, put horns in heads, rumple petticoats and beds, create suspicion among the innocent, upset a snob's headdress, or give a disease to a costive lap dog, only Spleen can fill Belinda with chagrin. Umbriel requests the goddess to do this.

Comment

This is a truly mock-heroic version of the traditional type of speech delivered to the gods in **epic** poetry. "Spleenwort" in line 56 was a mythical bough which was supposed to dispel the spleen, and it is used here to parody Virgil's *Aeneas*, who took a golden bough to grant him passage through Hades. Umbriel's address contains all the symptoms attributed to the spleen, such as melancholy, but Pope adds his own cynical touch when he includes such ailments as poetry and play writing. The "Headdress of a Prude" in line 74 is an ironical comment on the prudes of the day, who had borrowed the style of their hats from the Puritans.

Lines 79-88

Spleen pretends to ignore him, although in fact she grants his request. She binds together a bag like the one used by Ulysses to hold the winds, and in it she places the power of female lungs, sighs, sobs, passions and malicious gossip. She then fills a vial with fears, sorrows, griefs and tears. Umbriel takes the bag and happily carries it back to the everyday world.

Comment

Spleen's apparent refusal to comply with Umbriel's request, in spite of what she intended to do, is in keeping with the symptoms of the disease, spleen. The contents of the bag and vial are made ludicrous in comparison with the splendid booty described in the epics. The triumphant return to the world of mortals is also made in the true **epic** manner.

Lines 89-94

On his return to the world, Umbriel finds Belinda deep in the arms of Thalestris, her eyes downcast and her hair unbound. He opens the bag above her head, and all the furies are let loose. Belinda is immediately filled with superhuman rage, which Thalestris helps to increase.

Comment

The dejected portrait of Belinda in line 89 is adapted straight from Homer's *Iliad*. The Thalestris of mythology was an Amazon queen of great beauty and strength. In Pope's poem she probably represents the wife of Sir George Browne, cousin of Arabella Fermor's mother. Unbound hair in classical **epic** poetry always indicates anguish, and it appears as absurd here, considering the circumstances.

Lines 95-120

Belinda bemoans her fate, wailing at the thought of the preparation her hair had received, only to be defiled in this terrible way. She outlines the implements used in such preparation, like paper, torturing irons, hair fillets and lead weights. She dreads the thought of the stolen lock's being exposed to public view, where fops will envy it and belles stare at it. She pleads with the goddess "Honor" to forbid such a thing, and goes on to lament the loss of her reputation-a fate worse than death. She wonders how her honor can be restored and how she can prevent the lock from remaining in the lord's hands. Belinda ends her speech by exclaiming that the grass will grow in Hyde Park Circus; wits will take residence within the sound of Bow bells; earth, air and sea will fall in ruin; and men, monkeys, lap dogs and parrots will die first, before she will allow her reputation to be defamed.

Comment

This speech is delivered in the traditional **epic** style of the hero's angry response to an insult. Note that the implements used for setting hair are described as if they were implements of torture. In Belinda's speech to "Honor," Pope makes very clever and subtle use of **irony** inasmuch as everything, including virtue, is inferior to "reputation-which was sacred in 18th Century society circles. The word "Toast" in line 109 means a well-known woman, and the reference to grass growing in Hyde Park Circle is a comment on the dust there which was annoying to the beaux and belles of the day. And it would be unthinkable to have the fashionable. "Wits" living in the lower-class area of London signified by "Bow" bells (line 118).

Lines 121-130

On finishing her speech, Belinda rushes to her beau, Sir Plume, and asks him to retrieve the lock on her behalf. Sir Plume, who is extremely proud of his amber snuff box and clouded cane, addresses the lord in foppishly angry terms, and raps the box, presumably with the cane.

Comment

"Sir Plume" is Sir George Browne, husband of "Thalestris" mentioned above. His language here is that of the 18th Century dandy, and Sir Plume presents a ludicrous picture, particularly when he makes such a weak show of anger by rapping the snuff box. This was the passage which prompted Sir George Browne to threaten Pope with physical violence. Considering the poet's tiny stature and physical deformity, this suggests that Sir George was not exactly an **epic** hero. He withdrew his threats when someone pointed out that Pope would make a real laughing stock of him in print by way of retaliation.

Lines 131-140

The lord replies to Sir Plume that it grieves him to find such an articulate speech delivered in vain. He swears that the sacred lock will never return to the head whence it came, and thus it will forever adorn his hand. To make his point more emphatic, he triumphantly spreads out the stolen lock of hair.

Comment

The oath made by the lord is the true **epic** tradition, and Pope probably got his source from the *Iliad*. The "long contended Honors" in line 140 also comes from the classical **epic**. In the *Odyssey*, for example, Penelope is described as a "long-contended prize." When the prize is a lock of hair, however, the oath becomes absurd.

Lines 141-160

Umbriel, the malignant spirit, enters the story again by breaking Spleen's vial, from which sorrows flow. Belinda immediately begins to languish in grief, and, bathed in tears and with head drooping, she sighs and begins to speak. She curses the day she lost her beloved lock, and wishes she had never seen Hampton Court. Then Belinda consoles herself somewhat with the thought that she is not the first belle who has come to grief through loving Court life too much. She wishes she lived in some remote place where no coaches run, where Ombre is not played, nor tea drunk. Like a rose in the desert, she could bloom and die unseen in such a spot. She ends by cursing her thoughts for straying toward beaux, and wishes she had stayed home saying prayers.

Comment

Pope received his inspiration for Belinda's mournful speech from Achilles' lament in the Iliad, and he successfully maintains the same doleful tone throughout. In the *Odyssey* there are various references to remote isles of the kind Belinda craves so desperately. "Bohea" in line 156 was a type of tea drunk in fashionable 18th Century circles.

Lines 161-176

Belinda continues her speech by recalling the omens she experienced that some morning: three times her patchbox fell; her China shook, although there was no wind; even her lap dog, Shock, was rude. Then she remembers the warnings of the sylphs, and bemoans the fact that it is now too late. Wailing over the remnants of her once perfect hair and over the poor lock that now hangs without a companion, she threatens to remove it all. She wishes that at least the lord had removed hair that was hidden.

Comment

The use of omens, neglecting to obey them, and the curses of the heedless victim are all parts of the **epic** tradition which Pope is mocking here. Many of the references in this passage, including the "sacrilegious Hands" of line 174 and the addressing of the lord by the adjective "Cruel" in line 175, come from Virgil's *Aeneid*. The canto ends on a note of gloom and despair.

CANTO V

Lines 1-8

As Belinda finishes her speech, her listeners melt into tears-except the lord, whose ears have been stopped by fate and Jove. Thalestris reproaches him, but to no avail. Clarissa then waves her fan to get silence, and addresses the company.

Comment

Pope heightens the mock drama of his tale by making several classical **allusions** in this passage, all of them from Virgil's *Aeneid*. The character of Clarissa, the lady who lent the lord her scissors, was introduced to intensify the moral aspect of the poem. The speech she is about to deliver is a mock-heroic version of Sarpedon's address to Glaucus in Homer's *Iliad*.

Lines 9-18

Clarissa begins by asking why belles are praised more than anyone else for being angel-like, why beaux cluster round their coaches, and why they cause such a sensation in the theater. She says that such beauty is useless unless there is good sense to go with it, and claims that belles should aim at having men praise them for their virtue as well as their beauty.

Comment

Clarissa interprets the moral tone of the poem from the outset of her speech. This again is a mock version of similar lofty addresses in classical **epic** poetry. Philosophic praise of such qualities as the "good Sense" was a feature of 18th Century literary taste.

Lines 19-34

Clarissa says that if all-night dancing and dressing all day cured small-pox and warded off old age, housewifely care and learning useful things would be of no avail. It would be very pleasant if ogling, for example, produced saints, but unfortunately earthly beauty fades away and belles who despise men are doomed to dying as old maids. It is essential, she says, to use all one's faculties and retain good humor in spite of what we lose, because good humor can succeed to soothe a person when anger fails. She ends the speech by saying that belles may roll their eyes and charm with their beauty, but in the long run, only merit can win the soul.

Comment

Pope seems to lose his mock-heroic flavor momentarily in this section, and one gets the impression that he really means what he is saying. The reference to small-pox in line 20 is interesting and even rather poignant, since Lord Petre, the rapacious "lord" or "baron" of the poem, had died of the disease in 1713, the year before this version was published.

Lines 35-44

There is no applause for Clarissa's noble speech. Belinda frowns, Thalestris calls her a prude and calls everyone to arms. Everyone flies into the attack and there is a great deal of noise from fans, silks and whalebones. The heroes and heroines - the beaux and the belles - fight like the gods, unafraid of mortal wounds.

Comment

Clarissa receives no applause, compared to Homer's heroes, who are always applauded after delivering a speech. Note also the ludicrous weapons used in the battle, including the whalebones of petticoats, making this a truly mock-heroic **episode**. The very idea of fops and belles acting as **epic** heroes and heroines highlights the absurdity of the whole scene.

Lines 45-56

The fight is compared to one of Homer's battles on Mount Olympus, with the god Jove's thunder roaring throughout heaven and Neptune storming throughout the seas. The towers on earth tremble, the ground collapses and ghosts are alarmed at the break of day. Umbriel watches the fight from a sconce placed high on the wall, and claps his wings in triumph. Some of the sylphs watch the battle as they lean against bodkins, while others join in.

Comment

Pope definitely establishes the mock-heroic stature of the poem by introducing direct references to Homeric epics. The "Sconce" in line 53 is a candlestick attached to a wall, and the "bodkin" in line 55 is a blunt needle used for pulling tape through a loop. These four lines were added in this edition to keep the **epic** "machinery" of the sylphs in mind till the end of the poem.

Lines 57-66

Thalestris, the Amazon, flies through the battle and people drop dead at her glance: a beau dies with a **metaphor**; a wit with a song; two characters, Dapperwit and Sir Fopling, breathe their last, commenting on Thalestris' cruelty as they do so.

Comment

In this passage Pope successfully mingles **epic satire** with ironical comments on contemporary fashionable society. The names "Dapperwit" and "Sir Fopling" themselves are indicative of the types the poet is ridiculing, and are taken directly from characters in two popular plays.

Lines 67-86

Sir Plume pulls Clarissa down, but Chloe steps in and kills him with a frown. She smiles at her victory, but her smile brings

Sir Plume to life again. The god Jove sits in judgment on the case by weighing the wits of beaux against the lock of hair. The lock of hair wins. Belinda flies in rage at her enemy, the baron, who is not afraid of her. As they join in battle, Belinda takes some snuff between her finger and thumb and throws it in the lord's face. The spirits direct the grains to the target, and the baron sneezes loudly. Hampton Court echoes to the noise.

Comment

The device of using divine scales to measure human values is a popular device in **epic** poetry, and is found in the *Aeneid*, *Iliad* and *Paradise Lost*. Pope is here ridiculing the device itself as well as man's folly. Note the absurd nature of Belinda's victory. Sneezing in Greek and Roman times was considered an omen of good fortune.

Lines 87-102

Belinda shouts to the lord that he should be prepared to meet his fate, takes an ornament from her hair, and prepares to use it as a dagger. The history of this weapon is now outlined: her great-great-grandfather had worn it round his neck in the form of three seal-rings; when he died, his widow had it melted down and used it as a buckle; as a child, Belinda's grandmother used it as a whistle; her mother wore it in her hair as an ornament, and it is in this shape that Belinda uses it now as a dagger. The lord cries out that Belinda must not boast about his downfall, for she too will come to a bad end. He tells her not to think he is downcast at the thought of dying, but only at the prospect of leaving Belinda behind him. He therefore pleads with her to spare his life.

Comment

The life history of the hair ornament is outlined in mock-heroic style, with all the reverence of the classical **epic**. A similar passage is found in Homer's *Iliad*, in which the helmet's life story is traced. The lord's weak pleading here is a **parody** of the traditional gallant response of the **epic** hero in the face of death.

Lines 103-112

Belinda calls to the lord to restore the lock, and her cry echoes throughout Hampton Court. Even Othello did not make so much noise over the handkerchief that caused him grief. Yet often in such circumstances, there is so much arguing that the thing being argued about is forgotten. Everyone starts looking for the lock, but it cannot be found. Heaven decrees that no human being can be blessed with the lock, and no one dares argue against Heaven.

Comment

Pope uses exaggeration here to increase the dramatic tension and to sustain the mock-heroic effect. The "vaulted Roofs" in line 104 refers to the fact that the skies in classical **epic** poetry are often described as being vaulted. In Shakespeare's *Othello*, a handkerchief sets off the hero's rage, and Pope uses this

THE RAPE OF THE LOCK AND OTHER WORKS

reference here to make Belinda's disaster much more tragic than Othello's.

Lines 113-122

Some people thought the lock might have been taken to the moon, where things lost on earth are treasured. For that reason these items are found in the lunar sphere: heroe's wits kept in large vases; beaux locked in snuff-boxes and tweezer cases: broken vows, deathbed alms, and lover's hearts bound with ribbons; the promises of courtiers and the prayers of sick men; harlots' smiles and heirs' tears; cages for gnats and chains for capturing fleas; dried butterflies and books on philosophy.

Comment

Pope's list of absurd things to be found on the moon is very similar to a collection of items described by the Italian poet Ariosto in his famous poem, Orlando Furioso. The English poet here modernizes the list, however, and the hypocrisies and fopperies of the 18th Century are thereby ridiculed. "Dry'd Butterflies" are included in the list as an attempt to mock the natural history collections popular in Pope's day, and books on philosophy are there because the heavy type of philosophizing of the Middle Ages was unpopular among Augustans.

Lines 123-132

Suddenly the Muse of poetry spies the lock soaring upward to the skies, traveling too quickly for mortal eyes to see. Rome's founder also flew to the Heavens in the same way. The lock has changed into a star, and as it streams through the skies it is followed by a trail of shining hair. Not even Berenice's hair shone so brightly as Belinda's lock, and its flight is pursued by a train of attendant sylphs.

Comment

Pope again uses exaggeration to sustain the mock-heroic tone of the poem by bringing in classical references. Berenice was a character in classical mythology whose hair was changed into a constellation of stars. The sylphs were again brought into the poem in lines 131 and 132 to maintain the epic machinery.

Lines 133-140

The fashionable world will behold the lock from the Mall, and hail its progress through the skies with music. The lover will assume the lock to be Venus, and will dispatch vows to it from Rosamonda's lake. The wizard, Partridge, will himself examine the lock through "Galileo's Eyes," and he will then be able to forecast Louis' fate and the fall of Rome.

Comment

The Mall in line 133 was an enclosed walk in front of St. James' Palace, and Rosamonda's lake was a pond in St. James' Park. John Partridge was a contemporary stargazer who produced an annual almanac in which he always predicted the downfall of the Pope, and of Louis, King of France. "Galileo's Eyes" refers to the improved telescope produced by Galileo. This passage, almost at the end of the poem, brings us back to the ludicrous aspects of 18th Century life which Pope ridicules throughout his work.

Lines 141-150

Belinda is called upon to cease bemoaning the loss of her hair, which adds glory to the skies. She is assured that no mortal lock of hair can ever compare with the one which now shines above. After Belinda and millions of other people have died, she is told, her lock, consecrated to immortal fame by the Muse of Poetry, will inscribe her name forever among the stars.

Comment

Pope ends the poem on a note of **epic** exultation. Not only has the lock been translated into the heavens, but all the trivialities of society have been given almost divine significance by this act. The "Suns" in line 147 are Belinda's eyes, and the poem ends therefore as it began, since we were told at the beginning of Canto I that her eyes were brighter than daylight.

WINDSOR FOREST

INTRODUCTION

This is a descriptive poem written in the classical lyric style. A lyric is a poem for musical adaptation or accompaniment, expressing strong personal emotions. This poem was written in two parts, although in its finished form it is one complete whole. The first part was written in 1704, and the second in 1713, the year in which it was published. It contains certain passages - especially one describing the river Thames - which are attempted imitations of earlier models. Considering Pope was sixteen when he wrote most of it, *Windsor Forest* is a remarkably mature work.

Lines 1-6

The poem opens with an appeal to Windsor Forest, home of the monarch and the poetic muse, that it might inspire and receive his poetry. We are told that Granville has ordered it, and that the muse cannot possibly refuse his request.

> Comment

This is a traditional classical-type opening, with an invocation to the Muse addressed as Caryll was at the beginning of *The Rape of the Lock*. "Granville" is George Granville, who afterwards became Lord Lansdown. Pope dedicated the poem to Granville, who was himself a minor poet.

Lines 7-42

He compares the rustic scene with the Garden of Eden, claiming that Windsor Forest should be made just as famous. Everything here, he tells us, is "harmoniously confus'd." Slender trees stand around the chequered groves, and the poet can see "bluish" hills rising through the clouds. The purple health, the corn, and the green fields are blended to make the vista a most beautiful one. Even India with its exotic vegetation, and Olympus with its gods cannot offer anything more idyllic than this. The flocks, the flowers and the crops lend an atmosphere of peace and well-being to the rich land which is ruled by a Stuart.

> Comment

Pope is here employing the traditional method of exaggeration through comparison, in order to heighten his effect. Note the typical Augustan conception of natural beauty as being "harmoniously confus'd" - in other words, man imposes his order upon Nature's disorder to make it more beautiful. Line 38 is a thoroughly bad one, with grossly overdone effects obviously due to Pope's extreme youthfulness. The flattery to the Stuarts in line 42 also seems out of place, probably for the same reason.

Lines 43-64

This scenery was not always so beautiful. It was once barren and gloomy because of fierce animals and cruel laws laid down by royalty. He goes on to describe the savagery of the days when cities and countryside were laid waste. Famine stalked the land and men were treated on the same level as beasts because of the despotism of the times. As things got worse, men received worse treatment than beasts.

Comment

Pope blunders somewhat here in displaying a lack of historical knowledge, with resultant bad taste. The "savage laws" he talks of in line 45 were drawn up by the Stuarts, whom he has just praised. The remainder of this passage continues to display the exaggeration and lack of restraint which was absent in Pope's later poetry. Yet it shows that as a young man he was aware of and concerned about the suffering of those less fortunate than himself.

Lines 65-92

The fields lay bare and the cities were leveled, with winds blowing through the empty temples and deer wandering through the ruins. The tyrant, helped by the power of his nobles, held sway over the serfs and the Church with an iron rod. Yet the man who laid waste so much beautiful land was denied a burial when he died. The rulers who followed him heard the cries of the poor, and were pleased to see cottages being built in a peaceful atmosphere. Conditions began to improve generally, with flocks grazing again on the mountains and farmers working in the fields. Liberty, which is Britain's goddess, once more raised her head and looked to a happy future.

Comment

The description of devastation in this passage refers to the laying waste of the New Forest by King William I. The remark about the lack of burial in lines 79 and 80 alludes to the fact that when the King's body was about to be placed in its tomb in Caen, Normandy, a gentleman appeared on the scene claiming the place of interment as his inheritance. The picture of blissful peace he draws for us is, of course, as naive as his previous portrayal of desolation. Here again we can blame Pope's youth rather than his lack of judgment.

Lines 93-118

Pope calls on youth to go forth and make the best of the rural delights which Windsor Forest has to offer. He goes on to describe an idyllic hunting scene, and compares the capture of the quarry with Britain's conquering an enemy. He describes a pheasant rising, being wounded, and falling to the ground, then goes on to talk of the futility of the bird's physical beauty.

Comment

Comparing the hunting scene with Britain's militarism seems rather absurd, but we must again remember the fervent nationalism which probably affected the sixteen-year-old poet. He is probably referring here to the capture of Gibraltar by the British in 1704.

Lines 119-146

We are told of the beagles hunting the hare and the fowler roving the countryside in wintertime, when woodcocks are to be found in the glade. The fowler raises his gun, takes aim, and fires. Many lapwings and larks are shot in this way. The poet goes on to describe a fisherman watching the cork in the water, on the look-out for perch, eel, carp, trout and pike.

Comment

This passage shows that Pope as a boy had a normal, healthy interest in outdoor activities, and to a certain extent answers the criticism that the 18th Century was devoid of such interests. It also shows that "Nature" - in the sense of trees, flower, and so on-also had its appeal, even though this appreciation may have been expressed in a somewhat stilted or "unnatural" way.

Lines 147-170

Pope now describes the beginning of a hunting scene, when youths rush to cheer on the hounds and rouse the deer. The horses strain to get started, and when they do, the youths revel in the speed and excitement. Arcadia itself was not as beautiful as Windsor Forest, which can even boast its own goddess in the person of the queen. The queen guards the forest, and is the light of the earth and ruler of the sea. It is said that Diana herself wandered here once, and that her Virgins used to be seen on the lawn with bows.

Comment

In spite of rather absurd images like "sylvan war," Pope does succeed in capturing some of the excitement of the hunt in this passage. His flattery of royalty is again unnecessarily obtrusive, however, and he is once more guilty of exaggeration in his praise of *Windsor Forest*. "Arcadia" in line 159 was a mountainous region of ancient Greece noted for its pastoral beauty. The "queen" in line 162 was Queen Anne, and "Diana" in line 165 was the mythical goddess of the forests, often represented as a huntress.

Lines 171-218

The river Loddon is introduced now as "Lodona," daughter of the river Thames. She is described as a huntress. A belt is around her waist, a fillet is around her hair, and she carries a bow and arrow. She strayed from the forest once, and was seen by Pan, who pursued her "burning with desire." The pursued and the pursuer move swifter than eagles, until Pan is so close to her that she can feel his breath on her neck. Lodona pleads for help from father Thames and from Diana, but in vain. She prays to Cynthia, the moon goddess, that she wishes to weep and murmur in her native shades. Lodona now dissolves into what is still called the river Loddon, and continues to live in her native woods. In her "glass" can still be seen the skies and forests as she rushes into the Thames.

Comment

Pope's description of the river as a huntress is obviously influenced by similar passages in the ancient classics, but it is unsuccessful to the point of being almost incongruous. It is interesting to compare the style and content of this kind of passage with Pope's later poetry. The lack of balance and judgment here is in marked contrast to the polished control of his mature works. Lines 211 to 216 were added after the first version of the poem was published.

Lines 219-258

Pope now addresses the river Thames, who surveys the forest with its towering oaks. No sea, lake, or river can match the Thames for majesty, not even the River Po which has been praised so often by Latin poets. The stars themselves do not shine so brightly as the beauties that adorn the banks of the river Thames. Even Jove himself would be willing to exchange Olympus for a hill by the Thames. The man who loves this river is as happy as the man who loves his queen and country. Here a man can be inspired by his Muse, and become healthy from the herbs; he can consult the stars or indulge in scholarly activities; he can also reflect here, as well as seek spiritual solace. Scipio and Trumbal both retired to such an environment.

Comment

The poet's praise of the river's features is, of course, greatly overdone-to the point of embarrassment in places. Yet one can sense his youthful striving to achieve mastery over form and content, and to bring classical references into the poem without making them appear superimposed. The reference to Scipio and Sir William Trumbal in lines 257 and 258 allude to the fact that both men were forced into involuntary retirement.

Lines 259-290

He asks the Muses that he be taken to the banks of the Thames or to nearby Cooper's Hill, where he can be inspired by the beauty of the sounds. Denham and Cowley both received their inspiration here. The river even wept when Cowley's body was taken from the forest. The trees mourn the loss of the two poets, but now the poet Granville sings the forest's praises to make it immortal.

Comment

The address to the Muses again shows the classical influence on Pope, even at this early age. Sir John Denham and Cowley both wrote of this area, and were buried side by side in Westminster. This concludes the part of the poem written in 1704. The rest of the poem from line 291 to the end was written in 1713.

Lines 291-318

Surrey was also inspired by *Windsor Forest*, and was as successful with the pen as he was with the lance. It was here he wrote of Geraldine, just as Granville writes now of Mira. Pope goes on to talk of the heroes born here, such as Edward, and says that his heroic deeds against France should be immortalized in verse. The death of Henry should be mourned and palms should adorn his urn. The marble weeps for Henry, the martyr king, as Edward, who conquered everything from Belerium to the northerly sea, sleeps beside him. Both oppressor and oppressed lie side by side.

Comment

There is a marked change in direction in this passage as Pope starts making several historical references. "Surrey" of line 291 is Henry Howard, Earl of Surrey, who lived in Henry VIII's time and helped to refine English poetry. "Geraldine" in line 297 is the subject of a **sonnet** by Surrey, and "Mira" in line 298 is from one of Granville's poems. "Edward" in line 303 is King Edward III, and "Henry" in line 311 is Henry VI. Both Edward and Henry are buried in St. George's chapel, Windsor. "Belerium" in line 316 is Land's End, the most southern tip of England. At this point in the poem, Pope is obviously trying to introduce and develop a more philosophical and reflective tone prompted by the mood experienced at Windsor Forest.

Lines 319-348

Charles' tomb, obscure and uninscribed, should be made sacred. Pope proceeds to outline the miseries his country has seen through civil wars, and deplores the loss of life which has resulted from this strife. Finally Queen Anne ordered all fighting to stop, and peace followed. From this moment, father Thames proceeds to gleam and flow under the influence of the moon. Then his tributaries joined him-such as the rivers Isis, Loddon and Darent.

Comment

Charles I's grave is referred to in line 320 as obscure and uninscribed because from the Restoration until 1713 its exact location was unknown. In lines 327 and 328, Pope again indulges in some unnecessary flattery of Queen Anne. The list of rivers given between lines 340 and 348 are all rivers written about by the poets Spenser, Drayton and Milton. This whole passage shows a very conscious effort on Pope's part to introduce as many historical and literary references as possible.

Lines 349-384

The god of the river speaks now of the great fame that is due the Thames. No more shall rivers like the Tiber and the Nile be praised, now that the Thames has appeared. The Volga, the Rhine, and the Ganges are all associated with war, but the Thames will be renowned for peace. No more will British youths shed their blood in wars. Instead, they will spend balmy days hunting or tending their flocks. Works of peace will soar up on the banks of the Thames-villas, spires, and temples. A new Whitehall will arise, where Britain's fate will be decided, and where foreign kings shall beg to be allowed to kneel before the British Queen.

Comment

Several contemporary events are referred to in this passage: to the forthcoming peace settlement, for example, which was to take place at Utrecht: to the previous wars in Spain and Germany: and to the troubles surrounding the East India trading company. The "new Whitehall" in line 380 refers to the new palace designed by the architect Inigo Jones. Pope's contention that foreign leaders will beg to prostrate themselves before the British throne suggests a mild tendency toward chauvinism on the part of the young poet.

Lines 385-422

Windsor's trees will be turned into ships which will carry British thunder and religion to foreign parts such as Artic regions or tropical areas, where coral, rubies and gold are found. The "Unbounded Thames" will carry the uncouth ships of other nations, and "feather'd people," "Naked youths and painted chiefs" will flock to Britain to gaze, awed by its odd inhabitants. The forthcoming peace will bring back freedom to the Indians, kings to Peru, and gold to Mexico. Such evils as vengeance, terror and ambition will be banished forever.

Comment

The "Unbounded Thames" in line 398 refers to the hope that London would become a free port. The whole passage shows a certain wishful thinking on Pope's part, not untainted with some nationalistic fervor. Such boundless idealism is nevertheless refreshing in one so very young and so very English.

Lines 423-434

The poet ends with the wish that England's fame may be immortalized in verse. While Granville writes of gods, Pope's humble ambition is to propagate the atmosphere of peace which *Windsor Forest* has inspired in him. The young poet is satisfied if his words are heard only by the swains who inhabit the woods.

Comment

Pope attempts to crystallize for us here the lofty aim he had in writing the poem. In the classical tradition, it has a neat "rounding off" effect which counterbalances the invocation which opens the poem.

GENERAL COMMENTS

Cooper's Hill, a poem by Sir John Denham, is almost certainly the inspirational source of Pope's *Windsor Forest*. Denham's work is really the first example in English literature of what Dr. Johnson called "local poetry," an idea appealing to Pope although purely descriptive poetry was not a distinctive Augustan feature. The introduction of the river Thames, and its treatment as a person, is an attempt to imitate classical writers who had used this **convention**. One of the main weaknesses in the poem is the disorganized development of the historical **theme**. Compared to the poem *Windsor Castle* by Thomas Otway, another Augustan poet, Pope's work is historically weak and inaccurate. By 18th Century standards of lyrical poetry, however, *Windsor Forest* has a certain variety and dignity which make it unique.

MAN AND NATURE

Pope intends the forest to be universally symbolic of nature and man's place in it, which in turn leads him to expand his **theme** into one of historical prophecy. According to the poet, the forest is "Not Chaos-like," but is, "as the world, harmoniously confus'd." Man is therefore seen as being integrated with nature, encompassed by the wholeness of the universe. Pope achieves this integration by blending the general with the particular, hoping to capture the quality of a scene by outlining the details. General descriptions like "The bow'ry mazes, and surrounding greens," are mingled with more precise images, as in the line, "Thin trees arise that shun each other's shades." Notice in this last line the way in which the trees have individual identities within the over-all stillness. Also, when Pope talks about corn being "in waving prospect," we receive a particular image from a general abstraction. When Pope personifies an object in this poem, he tries to avoid a rigid effect by achieving the idea of a partnership between man and nature.

IMAGES AND LANGUAGE

Two short passages from *Windsor Forest* are worth studying in this respect; the one describing the fish between lines 141 and 146, and the other describing the reflections on water between lines 212 and 218. The first passage contains dazzling references to color outstanding in any poetic context. Adjectives and nouns are well placed, while phrases are skillfully contrasted: "bright-ey'd" and "shining," for example, run smoothly into "bedropp'd with gold" and "crimson." In the second passage on water-incidentally, probably the most beautiful in the poem-a feeling of calm is intermingled with a sense of vitality. "Headlong mountains" and "downward skies" fit in an atmosphere of "floating forests" which "paint the waves with green." None of the images are overdone or redundant, and the rhyming **couplets** help to maintain balance, control and harmony.

POPE ON WILD LIFE

Pope shows an appreciation of and sympathy with wild life in *Windsor Forest* quite remarkable in an Augustan poet. He deplores the killing of birds, for example, when he talks of the fowler roving with his "slaughterous gun," when "The clam'rous lapwings feel the leaden death" and the larks "fall, and leave their little lives in air." One gets the impression of the stark suddenness of death, together with a sense of irreparable loss. Pope also describes the excitement of animals vigorously and effectively when he talks of the spaniel "panting with hope," or the "impatient courser" pawing the ground, excited in "every vein." There is also a vitality about his animals - the beagles and the hare, for example - which fits perfectly into the tone and color of their natural environment.

MOTION IN THE POEM

The motion of the animals in *Windsor Forest* is also carried over into other areas, such as Pan's pursuit of Lodona between lines 171 and 218. In this passage, Pope captures the excitement and drama of the scene by interposing comparisons with birds, the sound of the footsteps, the panting of Pan's breath, and even the movement of his shadow as it is lengthened by the sun. The motion is continued when Lodona changes into a river which "For ever murmurs and for ever weeps." The emotions of nature, which marked Greek myth, are expressed perfectly in this passage with a fluidity which heightens the fusion of the natural and the human.

NATURE AND HISTORY

Various aspects of the forest are used symbolically to denote British historical features and characteristics - the oaks are "future navies," for example. A regal atmosphere is created when Windsor evokes the image of Queen Anne as a goddess who, as "empress of the main," protects the "sylvan scene." The Thames itself promotes an atmosphere of nobility, while, in a prophetic mood, the poet assures us that peace will reign when the "Unbounded Thames shall flow for all mankind." Note that there is an intended organic growth in the poem from nature, through wild life to thoughts on civilization. While Pope does not succeed completely in this aim - the "break" at line 290 is too noticeable, for example-he does manage to create a feeling of the limitless boundaries of art and nature. Imperial expansion is justified on the grounds that one's own country thereby becomes interlocked with other civilizations. But the forest also reminds Pope of historical wrongdoings, and between lines 43 and 92 we are given some account of the savagery and oppression contained in British domestic history.

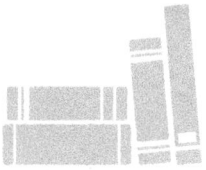

PASTORALS

| PASTORALS

A pastoral is a poem about shepherds and shepherdesses, dealing with their life and praising them for the work they do. Often a more serious theme lies beneath the surface, however, and we must bear this in mind when reading Pope's *Pastorals*. Written in 1704, when he was sixteen, and published in 1709, they are in four parts: "Spring" or "Damon," "Summer" or "Alexis," "Autumn or "Hylas and Aegon," and "Winter" or "Daphne." The background of these poems is in fact Windsor Forest, where Pope had gone to live at the age of twelve, but the poet use this setting only to gain universal effects.

| SPRING: THE FIRST PASTORAL, OR DAMON

The poem opens with an address to Sir William Trumbal, to whom this first pastoral is dedicated. Pope says that his Muse has inspired him in Windsor Forest, on the banks of the Thames, and hopes that England will resound to the sound of his poetry. He tells Sir William that the birds in Windsor Forest, where he was born, will rejoice that he is being so honored. He proceeds to tell how two shepherds, Daphnis and Strephon, and the muse, Damon, meet at daybreak and enter the following dialogue, which is paraphrased for the student's benefit:

Daphnis

Listen to the sound of the birds singing. Why do we sit here in silence, while the linnets greet the spring with their songs?

Strephon

Let us sing, then, and the Muse, Damon, will listen to us as the distant oxen labor in the fields. The crocus and violet are blooming, the breeze is blowing, and I will challenge you to a competition. I will stake that lamb over there, the one watching his reflection at the edge of the fountain.

Daphnis

I will stake this bowl, which is decorated with four figures representing the seasons of the year.

Damon

Start singing in order, just as the Muses sing. The hawthorn blossoms, daisies spring, leaves and flowers adorn the trees and ground, so commence, so that the valleys may echo to your song.

Comment

This opening is written in the classical pastoral way, with a dedication, two shepherds entering a dialogue and competition, and a Muse as arbitrator. Sir William Trumbal was a man fifty years Pope's senior, and it was he who had first seen the great merit of the Essay on Criticism. The pastoral setting is well established in these first few lines.

Strephon

I wish to be inspired with the works of Waller and Granville, in order that I may praise Delia. Then a white bull shall stand at your altars, threatening to fight and spurning the sand.

Daphnis

I want to win the prize for the sake of Sylvia, but I will not offer lambs or sheep as sacrifice. Instead, I offer my heart.

Strephon

Delia beckons me from the plain, then hides in the shadows to avoid me. She laughs to encourage my searching, but reveals her hiding place in so doing.

Daphnis

Sylvia trips gaily along the green fields, hoping really to be seen. She is running, but her eyes betray the fact that she wants to be caught.

Comment

Edmund Waller was born in 1605 and died in 1687. George Granville, who later become Lord Lansdown, was a poet who himself proposed Waller as his own model. The introduction of the lovers into the dialogue is another traditionally classic **convention** in the pastorals.

Strephon

Let the river Pactolus flow over golden sands, and let trees weep upon the banks of the Po. I nevertheless prefer the Thames, and would rather at end my flocks here than any other place.

Daphnis

Venus haunts Idalia's groves, Diana loves Cynthus and Ceres loves Hybla. If Windsor delights Sylvia, Cynthus and Hybla must yield to it.

Strephon

Nature is in mourning, the skies weep in showers, birds are silent and flowers close their petals. If Delia smiles, flowers bloom, skies brighten, and birds sing.

Daphnis

Nature is happy, the groves are fresh, and the sun is warming the air. If Sylvia smiles, new glories appear, and Nature is not charming in comparison.

> **Comment**
>
> Pope deliberately introduces classical references here by naming the two rivers. Note the competitive tone the dialogue has adopted, while the poem sustains its pastoral mood.

Strephon

In spring I love the fields, and in autumn the hills. In the morning I love the plains, and at noon the grove. But I love Delia always, and when I am away from her, neither plains nor groves delight me.

Daphnis

Sylvia is as ripe as autumn, as mild as May, brighter than noon, and as fresh as the early day. When she is absent, even spring does not please me, but when she is present, it is spring all year long.

Strephon

Tell me, Daphnis, tell me in what soil appears the tree that bears monarchs. Tell me this, and I will disclaim the prize, and give the honor to your Sylvia.

Daphnis

First of all, you tell me in what fields the thistle springs to which the lily yields. Do that, and I will ever hand over my charming Sylvia to you.

Damon

Stop this argument. Daphnis, I grant the bowl to Strephon, and you shall be awarded the lamb. Blessed are the shepherds whose nymphs excel in every grace, and blessed are the nymphs whose shepherds praise those graces in song. Haste now to those woodbine bowers which will guard you from sudden showers, while the flowers spread their fragrances around. For look! The flocks are gathering to seek shelter, and showers are beginning to fall.

Comment

The tree bearing the monarchs is a reference to the Royal Oak, where Charles II had hidden when he was pursued after the battle of Worcester. The thistle was the emblem of the Scottish Kings worn by Queen Anne, while the lily was the fleur de lis, the emblem of France. The resolution at the end of this passage is a common type of happy compromise employed by classical poets in pastorals.

SUMMER: THE SECOND PASTORAL, OR ALEXIS, LINES 1-22

This pastoral begins by describing a shepherd boy, Alexis, leading his flocks along the banks of the Thames. He is in mourning, and even the streams stop flowing in compassion. The shepherd asks Garth to accept his song, which tells what the unpracticed heart endures from love. The poem addresses the beeches and the streams, which can be defenses from the sun, but not from love. The woods shall answer, the hills and rocks will listen, but his loved one is too proud and hard to pay attention. The sheep bleat their sympathy, and the sun beats on the plain while his heart is full of winters.

Comment

This is a traditional type of opening for a classical pastoral lament on a "lost love" **theme**. Garth is Dr. Samuel Garth, author of the mock-heroic poem, *The Dispensary*, which influenced *The Rape of the Lock*. Line 16, "The woods shall answer, and their echo ring," is the **refrain** of Edmund Spenser's poem, *Epithalamion*.

Lines 23-48

Where have the Muses gone, while Alexis the shepherd pines away in hopeless love? Are they in the fields where the Isis glides, or in the valleys where the Cam flows? He looks in the water and sees his blushes, but they are of no avail, so he shuns the fountain. At one time, he knew all the herbs and plants that can cure lambs, but knows nothing that can cure his lovesick heart. Other shepherds may tend their flocks, but Alexis wishes to go to that fountain, where he can sing his song and embrace his love. He owns the flute that was Colin's when he was living, and which Colin bequeathed to Alexis when he died. Colin used to play tunes on it for Rosalinda, but now it hangs silently on a tree, despised by his beloved. He wishes that he were a captive bird within her bower, so that she would have to listen to him.

Comment

The proper name, "Colin", comes from Edmund Spenser's *Eclogues*, and "Rosalinda" is Colin's mistress. Note how continual references to rivers, mountains, trees and so on maintain the pastoral tone of the poem. Everything in the classical pastoral is related to some aspect of nature.

Lines 49-70

Yet his song is appreciated by the creatures of nature, for satyrs dance, Pan applauds, and nymphs leave their dwellings to bring gifts of fruit and turtle. But these gifts are given in vain, since Alexis merely bestows them on his beloved, together with a garland of flowers made by the shepherds. Great delights are to be found in sylvan scenes, where gods have found a heaven, where Venus and Adonis have wandered, and where Diana is to be found. Alexis asks her to share this delightful setting, where no viper is lurking, but where his love lies in wait for her. Bees sip the dew from blossoms here, but Alexis wants nothing sweeter than the one he loves.

Comment

The references in this passage to satyrs, Pan, nymphs, Diana the Huntress, and so on, blend the rural and classical atmosphere. The idea of begging one's love to share rural delights is a common device in ancient pastorals.

Lines 71-92

Alexis promises her that wherever she walks, cool breezes shall blow; wherever she sits will quickly become shaded; wherever she places her foot, flowers shall rise; and wherever she looks, things shall flourish. Alexis wishes she would join him, so that he could invoke the Muses and sing her praises in songs that would rival those of Orpheus. The forests, which are now wondering, would dance again, the mountains would hear him and the streams would listen as they fell. But he asks her to behold the shepherds shunning the noonday heat, the herds retreating to murmuring brooks, and the flocks moving to closer shades. He ends by comparing the coolness of the day, as the sun sets, with the fierce heat of his love.

Comment

The poet continues to sustain the complaining mood of the forlorn lover right to the end. Song, nature, and myth are all fused here to round off the over-all pastoral effect of the poem.

AUTUMN: THE THIRD PASTORAL, OR HYLAS AND AEGON, LINES 1-30

Pope begins by describing two shepherds, Hylas and Aegon, as they sing their songs in the shade of a beech tree. One of them mourns a faithless lover, Delia, and the other an absent lover, Doris. He dedicates his poem to Mr. Wycherley, who follows the art of Plautus and Terence with sense and humor. The poet asks him who is skilled in Nature to understand the passions and pains of swains who are in love. As the sun is setting, and clouds are streaked with purple, Hylas makes the rocks weep and the mountains groan with his song. Each section of Hylas' song is introduced with the **refrain**, "Go, gentle gales, and bear my sighs away" (or "along"), and he begins by comparing his pleadings to those of a sad turtle that has lost his love. He sings his complaint to the wind, hoping that Delia will hear him. The birds will stop singing for her, the lilies will hang their heads and die, and he ends by saying that absence is death to those who love.

Comment

William Wycherley was a writer of comedies with whom Pope struck up a friendship at an early age. In line 8, Pope makes a reference to Terence and Menander; by this he meant that Wycherley had joined Menander's comic spirit to Terence's art. The continual repetition of the **refrain** is reminiscent of Edmund Spenser.

Lines 31-54

He begins to curse the fields, blossoms and trees, but stops himself and expresses the hope that spring will attend Delia wherever she goes, flowers will bloom for her, and roses will adorn the oaks. Birds will stop their evening song, winds will no longer breathe, woods will not move, and streams will no longer murmur, before Hylas will stop loving. The sight of Delia is more preferable to him than fountains are to the thirsty swain, sleep to the laborer, showers to larks, or sunshine to bees. He begs her to join him, telling her that her name echoes through rocks and caves.

Comment

Notice the excessive reiteration of references to nature in this passage. Pope is determined here to relate every shade of emotion to nature, but tends to show a lack of judgment by excessive use of images.

Lines 55-84

Now Aegon calls upon the Muses for inspiration, and begins to speak. His complaint is about Doris, and as he speaks the mountains rise to the skies and the toiling oxen leave the pastures. Smoke rises from the villages, and shadows glide over the fields. He sees a distant poplar where they used to meet. He carved his vows of love there once, and Doris decorated the boughs with garlands, but now the vows have worn away and the garlands are faded. Fruits gleam on branches, grapes swell with wine, and berries paint the grove. He mourns the fact that all things bear fruit except his love. The other shepherds complain that Aegon's flocks are unattended, but he has no desire to tend sheep when his heart is broken. Pan came once and asked him what malignant eyes caused his grief. He answers that Doris' eyes can only bring him love.

Comment

The doleful tone is typical of classical pastorals of this nature. The reference to grapes is a particularly inappropriate one, since the location of the poem is Windsor Forest. Pope deliberately introduces references to the shepherds in order to sustain the traditional pastoral atmosphere.

Lines 85-100

He will run away from shepherds, flocks and plains. He will in fact forsake everything except love. He says he knows that love was born on foreign mountains, and was reared by wolves and tigers. Aegon bids farewell to the woods and the day as he threatens to leap from a cliff, so that his plaintive song will be heard no more. The pastoral ends with a description of the shepherds singing as the night fades, the dew falls, and the shadows lengthen.

Comment

The references to wolves and tigers add a romantic touch to the end of this pastoral. The threat of suicide is another **convention** taken from classical pastorals, as is the poignancy of the final scene, helped by the twilight atmosphere.

WINTER: THE FOURTH PASTORAL, OR DAPHNE

This pastoral, which was Pope's favorite, is dedicated to the memory of a Mrs. Tempest, who had died in a storm in 1703. It has its location in a grove at midnight, and takes the form of a dialogue between two swains, Lycidas and Thyrsis, which is paraphrased as follows:

Lycidas

Thyrsis, what murmuring spring does not sing as mournfully or as sweetly as you do. The moon is serene in the sky and the birds have forgotten to sing, so praise Daphne in song!

Thyrsis

Look at the groves shining with silver frost, all their beauty faded. Shall I try to copy Alexis' music that was heard by the Thames, who asked the willows on his banks to learn the song?

Lycidas

Just as the kind rains give moisture to the fields, give us music, and remember that the dying Daphne left instructions that we sing over her grave. So proceed, while I mourn beside her tomb and adorn her shrine.

Comment

The general tone of this poem is set from the beginning, and **allusions** are continually made to Mrs. Tempest's death. Note how nature and music again create the pastoral mood which is sustained to the end.

Thyrsis

Muses, leave your spring, and let nymphs and swains bring garlands. Hide the streams with myrtles, break your bows and inscribe this verse on stone with them: "Daphne is dead, so let nature and earth mourn." This is done, and you can now clouds dimming the day, trees weeping, and flowers dying upon the ground. What is the use of nature's beauty if Daphne is dead? For when she died, love died with her. In her memory, flocks refuse to eat, and swans sing in doleful tones. Sweet Echo lies silent in hollow caves, and answers only her name, for Daphne is dead, and all pleasure has gone. No dews descend from heaven, no odors arise from earth, there are no perfumes in the field, nor do herbs yield their fragrance. Zephyrs start blowing their laments, and bees neglect their golden store, since all sweetness is gone from the earth. When Daphne sang, larks would stop in mid-air to listen, birds would imitate her, and streams would stop their music - but no more, since she is dead. The trees hear of her death from a gentle breeze that blows, and the rivers overflow their banks with weeping. But look! Above the clouds and sky a bright light is shining, and eternal beauties fill the fields and groves! It is Daphne, and I beg her to look kindly upon us, and help us to grieve no more.

Comment

The expression "sweet Echo" in line 41 is taken from Milton's masque, *Comus*. In this passage, Pope brings the atmosphere of mourning to a **climax** in line 68 and creates a sudden change of mood reminiscent of the similar change at line 165 of Milton's lament, *Lycidas*. The poet is being thoroughly classical in every respect in this passage.

Lycidas

Everything is silent, intently listening to your song of woe. For you, Daphne, lambs shall often be sacrificed, and as long as plants cast shadows and flowers give odors, your name and honor will live on.

Thyrsis

Look, Orion sheds its dews, Boreas blows and Nature feels decay. Time conquers everything, and we must always obey Nature. Farewell, vales, mountains, streams and groves! Farewell, flocks and fellow shepherds, farewell, Daphne! I bid the world adieu!

> Comment

The pastoral ends on a classical note, and the last four lines contain **allusions** to the various subjects of all the pastorals and to the scenes which each one contains.

TREATMENT OF PASTORALS

Although it can be said that, in the true Augustan tradition, the theme of the *Pastorals* is man, it is nevertheless man at his weakest and most insipid. The men in these poems are pretty creatures with flimsy emotions, melodious tears and sickly smiles. Although they take place out of doors, the landscape is still too idyllic to be credible. Pope therefore dealt with this verse form in the same way as his gardeners treated his garden at Twickenham-he "methodized" it by smoothing the **diction** to satisfy the age's sense of elegance. If the landscape was wild, it had to be tamed; roaring torrents were turned into lisping streams; woods were seen at a distance, since gnarled trees were not aesthetically pleasing; and lawns had to be "velvet" and sheep "fleecy." In short, nature in Pope's hands was an imitation of art.

Theme Of Pastorals

When we think of a pastoral, we envision man working in a sunny atmosphere, usually tending his flocks. Life is apparently easy and simple, but classical pastorals demanded that man's problems and tensions be exposed more violently when placed in such a pleasing setting. Love, death, loss, desire are all treated within a natural framework in which all other turmoils have been silenced. That is why we have no howling gales, thunderstorms, or glowering mountains as a background, for all the raging and darkness is found in the hearts of the participants. This is in sharp contrast to the setting of the great scenes in Shakespeare's play, *King Lear*, for example, where man's anguish is heightened by placing him in a bleak, stormy setting.

GENERAL COMMENTS

Of these four pastorals, Summer and Winter are the best. Dealing with love and death respectively, they contain passages expressing poignant emotions which stand out from the rest in their sincerity and depth. Winter, for example, in mourning the loss of a loved one, contains a moving comparison of death and winter. Summer, on the other hand, contains lines in which the gentle tones of summer are placed in violent contrast to man's anguish. Note too that in all the pastorals, nature and poetry are both used to release emotional tensions - the shepherds all happen to be poets as well. What Pope is trying to do here is to create a balance between man and nature by placing season against season and love against death. He even employs the device of having one speaker counterbalance another in short lyrical passages - which we call "antiphonal speeches" - thereby creating the necessary poise and controlled effect. On the whole, however, it must be said that Pope seems to be more at home with **satire** than with pastorals.

ELOISA TO ABELARD

This poem, published in 1717 in a collected edition of Pope's work, is an epistle. An epistle is a poem written in the form of a letter, and the tone and content can be as varied as those of ordinary letters. Pope's poem is an expression of personal passion based on the 12th Century love story of Eloisa and Abelard, who chose love of God over love of each other. Abelard entered a monastery and Eloisa a convent, and it was from the cloistered seclusion of the convent that Eloisa wrote of the conflict between human and spiritual passion.

Lines 1-40

Eloisa asks herself why, in the cloistered solitude of the religious life, such a surge of passion should soar through her. She thought such an emotion was dead, but knows that it has been awakened by Abelard. She prays that she might never say or write his name, but his influence on her is too strong. She compares her coldness to that of the cells, chapels and walls of the convent, but she has not yet turned into stone. All her prayers to Heaven cannot completely shut out the memory of Abelard. As soon as she opened his letters, the name brought tears to her eyes, and prompts the thought that human love and desire for fame have been quenched in the convent.

Comment

Pope here uses the traditional opening of the classical epistle, in which the writer is struggling to reply to her lover's letter, usually accompanied by a display of emotion. Line 20 is borrowed directly from Milton's masque, *Comus*, while the image of the statues weeping in line 22 is taken from Virgil's *Aeneid*. "Fame" in line 40 really means "ambition," which Eloisa had at one time, since she apparently was renowned for her knowledge of languages.

Lines 41-80

She pleads that Abelard may write everything, and she will then be able to share his grief. All she can do now is read and weep, and begs Abelard to give her all his grief by letter. Letters were invented so that poor wretches like Eloisa can be comforted, and sighs can be heard "from Indus to the Pole." She reminisces on her first impression of Abelard, whom she regarded as almost an angelic creature. He taught her that it is no sin to love someone, and she does not envy the joy of saints when she remembers her happiness then. When thinking of marriage, she used to curse all laws not made by love. Fame, wealth, and honor mean nothing if there is no love.

Comment

The ideas of "th' all-beauteous Mind" in line 62 is a Platonic one developed more fully in Pope's *Essay on Man*. Eloisa is really using the argument here that true passion is defiled by worldly guarantees, and is deploring the action of women who consider marriage for its material benefits only. There is a moral tone here similar to that found in Clarissa's speech in the *Rape of the Lock*, Canto V.

Lines 81-128

When we scorn God's love, He jealously arouses emotions in us which make us seek in love things apart from love itself. Eloisa would turn down the world's greatest honor if she could become the mistress of the man she loves. When two people love, as she and Abelard did once, they find the true freedom of nature in such a relationship. She now breaks into a cry of anguish over the way fierce, uncontrolled passion brought violence and shame to their love. She immediately recollects her decision to enter the religious life, and remembers kissing the veil as she made her perpetual vow. She admits, however, that her thoughts were not on the Cross, but on Abelard, and she goes on to beg him for his passionate love. But suddenly she breaks off and prays that she be able to banish thoughts of Abelard and dedicate her life to God.

Comment

Some of the views expressed here on love, liberty, nature, and law are developed more fully in Pope's *Essay on Man*. The word "pain" in line 104 means "punishment" as well as having the usual meaning. Abelard was apparently present when Eloisa professed her vows. The line "Still drink delicious poison from thy eye" is borrowed from Shakespeare's *Antony and Cleopatra*.

Lines 129-170

She tells him that the nuns deserve a letter from him, and goes on to describe how he founded the convent and made a spiritual oasis in the wilderness. But the nunnery is bleak without Abelard's influence, and even her prayers have proved of no avail. He is a father, brother, husband, and friend all in one, and all the physical beauties and serenity of the place do not compensate for him. In his absence, a mood of dark melancholy prevails which is felt everywhere.

Comment

The idea of an oasis suddenly springing up is found in Milton's *Paradise Lost*. The idea is stressed here that the convent was built from love and not from the money of usurers. The phrase "visionary maid" in line 162 means a "maid who sees visions." "Isles" in line 164 means the aisles of a church. Note the powerful poetic image, from line 165 to 166, of the goddess Melancholy spreading her dark wings over the cloistered scene.

Lines 171-206

She must stay here, however, until she dies, for only death can break the vows she has taken. The basic conflict, love of God against love of man, is expressed now, and Eloisa prays for guidance. She does not know, however, if her prayer is one based on piety or on despair. Even in this cold, chaste atmosphere the forbidden fires of passion can spring up, and she is aware of her crime while unable to feel really guilty. She asks how she can possibly loathe the offense, yet love the offender, and proceeds to show that all the regrets and repentance still cannot make her forget. She begs that she may be able to banish thoughts of Abelard forever and think of nothing but God.

Comment

The central **theme** of the Epistle is outlined in this passage, which is a poignant expression of the tension created between physical and spiritual passion. "Confess'd" in line 178 is used in both the ordinary and the religious sense. The idea is developed that to forget one's love for someone is the cruelest form of penance, and the most difficult one to execute. "Sense" in line 191 means sensation as well as perception. The end of this passage contains the essence of medieval mysticism, namely the total renunciation of the flesh and total immersion in the Spirit.

Lines 207-248

The Vestal is to be envied, since her mind is spotless, all her prayers are answered, and her mind and spirit are perfectly composed. She is bathed in grace, she lives in an eternal Eden, and white virgins sing hymns for her. When she dies, heavenly harps play. Eloisa has other thoughts that trouble her, however, for at the close of day Abelard is always in her mind. Strange demons torment her, rousing deep passions which make her want to clasp his memory. When she awakes, however, these thoughts have gone, so she closes her eyes and imagines she sees Abelard beckoning to her from the skies. Winds and waves roar, she shrieks, wakes up, and finds he is not there.

Comment

The beginning of this passage is a poignant expression of envy for those who have never experienced physical love. Pope probably borrowed the idea of Eloisa's reliving experiences in dreams from Chaucer and Dryden, both of whom has used this **convention** in their poetry. The word "conscious" in line 229 has a dual meaning: it implies the night's sharing knowledge as well as Eloisa's awareness of her feelings during the night.

Lines 249-276

Eloisa says that Abelard has a comparatively easy time, inasmuch as his denial of earthy pleasures in itself soothes the wounds of his soul, whereas she has fierce passions to contend with. Abelard had nothing to lose by helping her, and she craves his help. The memory of him continually comes between her and the execution of her religious duties, while her soul burns with passion for him, conflicting with her love of God.

Comment

The reference to the eternal flames burning in tombs is a common one in medieval literature. Eloisa says that her tears are "too soft" in line 270, because they are tears of love, not of contrition. This is a strongly evocative passage, again demonstrating the unbearable tension between love for God and passion for man.

Lines 277-316

While Eloisa is prostrate with grief, she begs Abelard to visit her, as only he can dispel her gloom. She even asks him to help tear her from God, but immediately changes her mind, telling him to cut himself off from her forever, so that she can devote herself to the spiritual life. In this mood, she bids farewell to him and looks forward to a life of eternal peace. She then has a vision of herself being called to eternity by the dead.

Comment

This passage indicates the fierce internal debate that Eloisa is having with herself, and the tension which is almost unbearable. The phrase "low-thoughted care" in line 298 is from Milton's *Comus*, and several phrases in this passage are borrowed from Dryden.

Lines 317-342

She continues her reverie about death, saying that Abelard will be there when she dies, and will give her the last rites. He will present the Cross before her eyes, and on that last occasion it will be no crime to see Eloisa, as it is now. Death will have conquered, and Abelard too will one day find eternal peace among the angels.

Comment

There are several passages in Virgil's *Aeneid* similar to this one. The image of Eloisa sucking her last breath (in line 324) is also found in Virgil, Marlowe, and Dryden. Eloisa here is saying virtually that life without Abelard is unbearable, and that death will be a happy release from the pain she is suffering.

Lines 343-366

Eloisa ends with the hope that they will be buried together in one tomb, and she foresees the day when two lovers might gaze upon their joint grave with the hope that their love will not end the same way. She also wishes that if some future poet hears of them, he will immortalize their story in song.

Comment

Eloisa and Abelard were actually buried together in the Monastery of the Paraclete, he having died in 1142 and she in 1163. The last few lines of the poem are really directed to Lady Mary Montagu, a lady for whom Pope had formed an attachment. The phrase "whole years in absence" in line 361 refers to the fact that she was in Turkey at the time the poem was written.

FORM OF THE POEM

Eloisa to Abelard is an epistle, a form of poetry which Pope set out to master in the true classical tradition. The model to whom he turned for inspiration was the Latin poet, Ovid, whose epistles, the Heroides, had long been the object of translation, imitation, and even **burlesque**. Chaucer himself translated passages from Ovid's epistles and included them in his own poem, the Legend of Good Women. As time went on, the letters of *Eloisa to Abelard* were losing their medieval tone in the process of transposition-particularly in French literature - and in England a translation appeared in 1713 by a John Hughes, with whom Pope corresponded from 1714 until Hughes' death in 1720. Pope's poem brought the epistle form of poetry back into line with Ovid's rules, namely that the characters had to be historical and that the woman had to be deserted by a man.

THE HUGHES TRANSLATION

Pope used this translation to get the **theme** of his poem and the form in which it was expressed. Hughes provided Pope with all the details he required, although there was much in the Hughes translation that Pope had to change and reject. Hughes wrote the letters in prose, for example, and misses much of Eloisa's passion-he even makes her say at one point, "I had Wit enough to write a Billet-doux." Pope avoids this type of absurdity, and captures much of the passion and anguish which Eloisa felt. Hughes also makes Eloisa waver in her decisions from time to time, whereas in Pope's poem the major decision has been made. She is a nun still physically in love with Abelard; and the only choice she has is either total immersion in her vows or death itself.

RHETORIC AND EMOTION

The rhetoric of Pope's poem has often been criticized, and the emotion has often been described as shallow and insincere. The rhetoric, however, is justified inasmuch as the historical basis of the poem had already been established. The reader already knows the story and the outcome, so a rhetorical epistle is the most dramatic way of expressing the point of crisis. The audience wants to read a poignant version of the tragedy, and the writer satisfies his audience in letter form. In so doing, he delves into the past by outlining present emotions. These emotions are not only those of the letter writer, but those of the audience as well, and it is the poet's task to manipulate them as skillfully as possible. The emotions in this poem are, in fact, part of Nature, the only thing "unnatural" in the circumstances being that Eloisa's love is a dual one, and is in fact incapable of being resolved except by the methods already outlined.

GENERAL COMMENTS

Eloisa to Abelard is a poem unified by Eloisa's passion, by which she makes religion into an erotic fantasy - and she even makes death a lover's tryst. There is also a remarkable variety of pace in the poem, from reflections on mysticism to expressions of passionate physical devotion. The poem was published in Pope's collected works of 1717, but he had mentioned it earlier in a letter to Martha Blount, toward whom he felt great affection. His emotions changed, however, and by 1717 he was attached to Lady Mary Montagu, to whom he in fact addresses the last few lines of the poem.

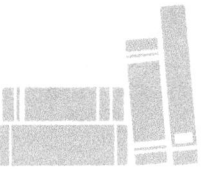

OTHER WORKS

ODE ON ST. CECILIA'S DAY

An ode is a lyric poem which is very exalted in tone, demonstrating great enthusiasm for its subject matter. This poem was written by Pope in 1708 at the request of the essayist, Steele, and is in praise of music. Although it was not universally greeted as one of his best efforts, Pope's poem was itself set to music much later and even given a public performance in 1730. For this musical version, Pope made several minor changes in the original poem, and even added an extra stanza.

THE DYING CHRISTIAN TO HIS SOUL

This poem is also an ode and, like *Ode on St. Cecelia's Day*, it was written at the request of the essayist, Steele. In the letter which Pope sent to Steele with the poem, the poet says he wrote it on a sudden inspiration prompted by some verses by the Latin poet, Hadrian, and Sappho. It has been noted, however, that this small poem bears a strong resemblance to an ode by an obscure earlier poet called Thomas Flatman. Written in 1712, it is interesting both from a structural and religious point of view, and is remembered particularly for its last line.

Elegy To The Memory Of An Unfortunate Lady

An **elegy** is a poem written as a lament for the death of someone and usually contains grave philosophical meditations. This poem, published in 1717, has caused some controversy due to the identity of the "Unfortunate Lady." She was almost certainly a Mrs. Weston, a friend of Pope's with whom he corresponded for several years, but in any case the poem can be read as a purely imaginative work. It was criticized by the great Dr. Johnson as being a defense of suicide, but this seems an extremely unwarranted accusation. The poem is notable for the pathos it demonstrates.

THE UNIVERSAL PRAYER

Published in 1738, this poem has been described as a paraphrase, or a restatement, of the Lord's Prayer. A reading of the poem, however, shows that this is not so, although the opening and the last four **stanzas** are obviously influenced by it. Many of Pope's contemporaries called this poem a "Deist's Prayer," and when it was translated into French, the translator was severely criticized for propagating unorthodox religious views. The Universal Prayer can in some ways be regarded as Pope's personal commentary on his own *Essay on Man*.

POPE AS A CRITIC

Pope And Homer

As we have already seen, Pope achieved fame and fortune with his translations of Homer's *Iliad* and *Odyssey*. The student will also have noticed the great number of references to Homer throughout Pope's great poem, *The Rape of the Lock*. Why was this? What particular appeal did Homer have over any other classical poet? To begin with, Homer was considered a "practical" poet, an artist of common sense and "judgment" who satisfied all the 18th Century demands for such qualities. More than that, however, his qualities and achievements as a poetic artisan appealed to the Augustans in general and to Pope in particular because of his power of "invention." In Homer's time, poetic standards were not very high, and he did a great deal to bring poetry - and particularly **epic** poetry - to a lofty artistic level. He drew on ancient myths, for example, to improve his "machinery," such as gods; he turned simple legends into profound and meaningful allegories; he even introduced political philosophy into the moral of his writings. From this alone, then, we can understand the appeal he had for Pope, particularly since Homer set a tone for **epic** poetry which was timeless and a form which was as valid in the 18th Century's Age of Reason as it was in the heroic age of ancient Greece.

Pope And Le Bossu

In Pope's day, writers often turned to the great French critic, Le Bossu, for the rules and canons of their craft. One of Le Bossu's ideas was that a writer had to think of a moral first, then supply the story to fit it. In view of his knowledge of Homer, Pope was severely critical of Le Bossu for this view, and went as far as to ridicule the Frenchman in his Recipe to Make an **Epic** Poem, which was published in the periodical, the Guardian. If a poet followed Le Bossu's rule, said Pope, an **epic** poem could be written virtually without talent or study.

In his essay, Pope outlined techniques for employing **epic** "machines" and showed the best ways of using myths and allegories. Pope agreed that a critic should demonstrate the abstract rules which are embodied in a work of art. This did not mean, however, that a poet could write a poem just by applying some rules. A knowledge of Aristotle and Le Bossu certainly helps, but Pope's claim was that learning and genius were also required. Furthermore, the question arose of whether the rules that applied to ancient Greece could also apply to 18th Century England. Pope indeed tried an original, full-length **epic** apart from his translations, but it was never completed. From what we have seen of 18th Century taste and sensibility, it would appear that the age was not exactly suited to the sweeping themes and grand aims of the epic.

Pope And Imitation

"To follow Nature" was, as we have seen, one of the golden rules of the 18th Century. It was an ancient rule, however, and 18th Century poets "imitated" the ancient poets just as Virgil had imitated Homer. We must not exaggerate Pope's debt to classical poets, however. He imitated them, to be sure, but always with the aim of developing himself fully as an Augustan poet. Also, while he turned to Continental poets more than to his own English predecessors, his poetry does show the marked influence of writers like Chaucer, Dryden and John Donne. Pope was humble enough, then, to admit his debt to classical writers, both ancient and modern, but he always took elements from them into his own creed. He always had his own opinions about poetry and followed them first and foremost. From the emotional point of view, Pope certainly "held back" in such poems as Eloisa to

Abelard, but he did so quite literally to meet Virgil's standards more than anything else. Pope fell heir to the tradition of narrowing the range of emotional expression in poetry, but did so only because this idea fitted into his own critical conception of what true poetry should be. The student should always bear in mind the fact that Pope, despite his critical theorizing on imitation, following Nature in the classical way, and so on, was in all ways a thoroughgoing poet of his own age.

ESSAY ON CRITICISM

Written when he was only twenty, this poem is often compared to a work by the Latin poet Horace called *Ars Poetica*, and Boileau's work, the *Art Poetique*. It was immediately hailed by his contemporaries, including Addison, as a masterpiece. The poem is divided neatly into three parts: the basis of criticism, the causes that prevent criticism, and finally, the causes that produce criticism. In this poem, Pope sees a connection between the revival in the art of criticism and the great revival of learning known as the Renaissance. Yet it is not a treatise on the art of poetry as such, but rather a discussion on criticism as an art in itself, in which comments on poetic criticism naturally had their place. It is not a complete success as a poem, mainly because there is no central idea developed, and the transitions from thought to thought are extremely abrupt. The precepts themselves, however, are expressed neatly and "wittily." The topics covered in the work include such things as the limitations and study of taste; nature considered the best guide of judgment; critics in wit, language and versification; rules for the conduct of manners in a critic; the character of an incorrigible poet and that of an impertinent critic.

ESSAY ON MAN

Written in four epistles as part of a large, projected scheme which was never completed, Pope's Essay on Man nevertheless stands as a work in itself.

First Epistle

This deals with Man and his place in the universe, and contains a defense of the divine wisdom which created man and placed him on earth. Any inquiry into man's place in the universe is hampered, however, by our limited knowledge of the world. What we do know, however, is that there is a graded scale of beings, and that man is an imperfect part of a divine and perfect Order.

Second Epistle

This develops the argument that even with his failings and imperfections, man can still fulfill his divine function. Man can and may analyze this unique role, but he cannot ever "scan" God. There are two principles in human nature that always fight for supremacy: the first is stimulating self-love and the other is restraining reason. Above all, God is working out His divine scheme for man.

Third Epistle

This concentrates on the thesis that the purpose of divine rule is to sponsor the general good, although man is so limited that he cannot always see how this is being accomplished. The main argument here is to prove that in God's scheme of things, self-love and reason work to the same end, namely the propagation and achievement of universal good.

Fourth Epistle

This outlines the application of the general principles contained in the whole work. The divine scheme being perfect, it is therefore aimed at happiness for everyone; happiness is therefore a general quality, but one dependent on particulars. God has granted to every man the means toward the attainment of happiness. The poem ends with the idea of the fundamental benevolence of the universe.

THE RAPE OF THE LOCK

CRITICAL COMMENTARY

GENERAL COMMENT

As we have seen, Pope's contemporaries, on the whole, held him in the highest esteem as the greatest Augustan poet. When his poem, *The Rape of the Lock* was translated into French and Italian, he was hailed throughout the Continental literary world as the leading English poet of his day. After his death, however, controversy raged over his poetic stature, and estimations of him have ranged from adulation as a genius to dismissal as a charlatan. Here the student has a brief summary of some critical opinions on Pope, some dealing with his poetry in general, and others with specific poems.

WARTON

Joseph Warton in his *Essay on Pope* (1757) attacked Pope for having greatly overdone moralizing in verse. He even went so far as to say that Spenser was a greater poet than Pope, a judgment which was closely to heresy in the 18th Century.

Warton's contemporaries were so shocked, it is said, that he did not dare publish anything else for many years.

COLERIDGE

Samuel Taylor Coleridge (19th Century) complained strongly of Pope's ideas on Nature, saying that if we try to analyzed Nature by reason alone, it becomes something cold and factual. He criticized Pope for omitting the elements of mystery in Nature, making it an object of intellectual study and not of emotional rapport.

PATER

Walter Pater (19th Century) criticized Pope for his "exquisite insipidity."

STRACHEY

Lytton Strachey (19th Century) praised him highly, saying that he "turned his screams into poetry, with the enchantment of the heroic couplet."

ELVIN

The Reverend Whitwell Elvin (19th Century) was one of the leading Victorian critics of Pope's works. His attacks were as venomous as Pope's were at the poet's most bitter moments, although the cleric did not have the Augustan's brilliant wit.

ARNOLD

Matthew Arnold (19th Century) damned Pope with faint praise, saying that he was a classic writer-of prose, not of poetry. The implication here is, of course, that Pope cannot be considered a poet at all.

BYRON

Lord Byron (19th Century) showed a reverence for Pope's poetry, and his reasons for this are worth examining. He regarded his own work as positively tawdry in comparison, without ever considering that his outlook and talents were different from those of Pope. He went so far as to look on Pope as mankind's universal poet. In the Augustan's poetry, Byron found the harmony, passion, sense and invention which he wished to achieve in his own. Byron also praised Pope for his wealth of imagination, and in 1821 wrote in a letter: "I will show more **imagery** in twenty lines of Pope than in any equal length of quotation in English poesy." He also admired the Augustan for the moral worth of his poetry, and for the aristocratic tone maintained in it. Byron held Pope up as someone to be copied, in contrast to what he called the "vulgarity" of "the new school of poets."

SITWELL

Dame Edith Sitwell (20th Century) was an outstanding champion of Pope and his poetry. It is very interesting to note that she was one of the earliest sponsors of Dylan Thomas' poetry as well - and no two poets ever had less in common than Pope and

Thomas. She did criticize Pope for his vanity, however, which she said was "the one grave fault in his character."

AUDEN

W. H. Auden in *Essays in Criticism* (1951) considers two generally held opinions on Pope, namely that his poetry is either "falsely poetic" or that it is cold and without emotion. He answers these two criticisms by pointing out that Pope and the Augustans were interested in a different kind of "Nature" from that of the Romantics. Pope's descriptions of rustic scenes were perhaps vague, but his outline of Belinda's boudoir wasn't, because the Augustans focused their attention on things that did not interest someone like Wordsworth. Pope was certainly not a dramatic poet, but he did write from his own experience, and this experience was crystallized with a fusion of vision and language which few poets can rival. When Pope wrote in the preface to the *Odyssey*, for example, that "There is a real beauty in an easy, pure, perspicuous description even of a low action," he was saying exactly what he meant, and put it into practice.

LEAVIS

F. R. Leavis in his *Revaluation* (1947) pointed out that the lofty formality of Pope's poetry was natural to him because it was sanctioned by his contemporaries. The "correctness" of his works was an aspect of the civilization to which the poet adhered, and what may appear superficial to us was "Reason" and "Nature" to the Augustans. The 18th Century stood for codes which seem narrow and less subtle when compared to other ages, but on the other hand it received its strengths and concentrated purpose from these conventions. Pope was indeed as insolent as often as he was elegant, but he was never inane. He was essentially a poet of substance, and we find the most striking evidence of this in his satirical passages. Pope was also a master of the Grand Style, and here again the period supported such a **convention**. He also holds the key poetic position between the 17th and 18th Centuries.

MONK

Samuel Holt Monk in the *Journal of the History of Ideas*, Vol. 5 (1944) tells us that when Pope employed such terms as "nameless graces" and "a grace," he was using the jargon of aesthetics, and the word "grace" in a critical sense is one which crops up in 17th and 18th Century criticisms. It is an important concept, and one which goes a long way to clarify for us Pope's views on poetry. There were really seven aspects to Pope's definition of grace: (1) it had a definite aesthetic quality; (2) it was one of nature's gifts; (3) it must be distinguished from beauties which rules make possible; (4) it has a sudden, surprising effect; (5) it cannot be analyzed; (6) its appeal is more to the heart than to the head; and (7) it is notably the mark of genius. In this respect, Pope notes in his *Essay on Criticism* that rules are not enough for poetic effects, thus making room for poetic license and originality.

WARREN

Austin Warren in his Rage for Order (1959) shows that Pope's poetry develops from the elegant and decorative to the rich and grotesque mode of expression. There was a variety in his poetry which is seen if we compare, say, his *Pastorals* with his essays on *Man and Criticism*. He believed in variation within the framework of "pure" poetry, which also had to be musical. And to Pope, there were many kinds of poetic music ranging from the gentleness of the *Pastorals* to the majesty of his Homeric translations. While his poetry has been praised and blamed for its "smoothness," its "sweetness," or its "melody," we should not forget what Pope himself said in this respect: "I have followed the significance of the numbers, and the adapting them to the sense, much more even than Dryden; and much oftener than any one minds it." What Pope really means is that a poem's meaning is inclusive of its sound as well as its statements that can be paraphrased.

WIMSATT

W. K. Wimsatt, Jr. in the *Modern Language Quarterly*, Vol. 5 (1944), outlines the relation of **rhyme** to reason in Pope's poetry. Many examples of Pope's **rhymes** are given to show how Pope takes more advantage of the quality of **rhyme** difference than most poets. He is consequently one of the great rhymers in English poetry. Pope's rhyming is contrasted to that of Chaucer, who himself had found a scarcity in rhyming words. The problem was even more acute for Pope, since English had lost many of its easy **rhymes** in the course of three hundred years. The Augustan therefore rhymed words which had much wider meanings than those used by Chaucer, and Pope's couplets, unlike Chaucer's, are characterized by unity, intellectual clarity, and a sense of "completeness." Pope's **rhymes** are also marked by difference in parts of speech or in the usage of the same part of speech. **Rhyme** in Pope is a perfect fusion of sound and sense.

WILLIAMS

Aubrey Williams in the *Philological Quarterly*, Vol. 41 (1962) points out some of the parallels between Milton's *Paradise Lost* and Pope's *The Rape of the Lock*. (1) The dream of pride whispered into Belinda's ear is reminiscent of the dream insinuated into Eve's ear in Books V and VI of *Paradise Lost*. (2) The boudoir scene in which Belinda worships herself recalls Eve's admiration of herself as mirrored in the pool of Eden. (3) Ariel searching "the close Recesses of the Virgin's Thought" before the cutting of the lock reminds us of the helplessness of the Angels in the face of man's free will.

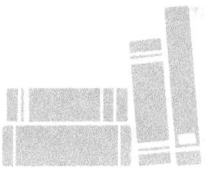

THE RAPE OF THE LOCK

ESSAY QUESTIONS AND ANSWERS

Question: What characteristic elements of 18th Century poetry are evident in *The Rape of the Lock*?

Answer: This poem is typical of Augustan poetry in many respects. It obeys the rules which the age laid down for taste, judgment, nature, imitation, wit, poetic form and **satire**. The poem is classical in taste, drawing on the best elements of ancient poetry and fitting them into Pope's views on contemporary man. It was written in the true humanistic spirit of the age, by which man was examined in the light of the classical past. The poet's sense of judgment is displayed by the skillful way in which he inflates a trivial incident to **epic** proportions and deflates epic machinery to ludicrous dimensions. He demonstrates these skills, for example, by the very fact of making this absurd event the subject of a poem and by transforming the epic gods of old into delicate 18th Century sylphs. The poem deals brilliantly with what the Augustans meant by "Nature," inasmuch as it gives a general picture-albeit a gently ironical one-of the customs and mannerisms of contemporary society. It does so, however, by describing and commenting on the minute details of that society, such as Belinda's boudoir or Sir Plume's snuff box. By so doing, the foibles of the age are magnified and satirized more deftly than has ever been done in any similar poem in English literature.

The Rape of the Lock is also outstanding for the "wit" it contains. "Wit" in the 18th Century meant, of course, saying something as cleverly and sharply as possible, but the poem is outstanding in the modern sense of the word too. Sometimes Pope embraces both meanings of "wit" in one line with devastating effect, as in his comment on the Queen's taking advice and tea at Hampton Court. From the aspect of imitation, the poem fulfills all the demands of the age inasmuch as it is filled with classical **allusions** re-created in a contemporary setting. Every page of the poem abounds in "remodeled" phrases, passages and personages from Homer and Virgil, for example, as in the whole description of an **epic** battle in the form of a card game. The entire poem translates for us the total mood and tone which we associate with classical poetry, and this complete transference of effect was in fact the essence of Augustan "imitation." Technically, Pope has given us virtually a flawless example of 18th Century poetic form. The work is written entirely in heroic couplets, each one economically fashioned with stylish phraseology, neatly turned witticisms, and pungent observations-all the prerequisites of Augustan verse.

But it is the satirical aspects of the poem that establish its position as one of the outstanding works in English literature. **Satire** was highly regarded in the 18th Century, when figures like Swift and Addison made penetrating, amusing, and sometimes biting commentaries on many features of their society. Pope, using the mock-heroic techniques established by the ancients and developed by the Frenchman, Boileau, and the Englishman, Garth, captures and mimics in this work all the aspects of classical **epics** and contemporary life which he thought worth satirizing. It can be safely said that *The Rape of the Lock* is a poem highly characteristic of Augustan poetry in its polished treatment of **theme**, economic enrichment of topic, and elegant enlightenment of vision.

Question: Discuss the use of classical **epic conventions** employed by Pope in the poem.

Answer: In the true Augustan tradition, Pope looked to the classics, such as Virgil's *Aeneid* and Homer's *Iliad* and *Odyssey*, as models to be imitated. Since *The Rape of the Lock* was a mock-heroic poem, he obeyed one of Le Bossu's cardinal rules by including in its structure as many classical epic **conventions** as possible. In Canto V, for example, he borrows the idea of the **epic simile** (i.e., the comparison of one item or event with a long list of others) when he relates the **catastrophe** in Hampton Court to some great occurrences in Homer's poetry. Much of the traditional machinery used in classical **epics** is also found in Pope's poem. The fate of Helen of Troy itself is being mimicked by the very title and subject matter of the poem, while the great feasts described by Homer become the 18th Century ritual of pouring coffee. The huge shield carried by Achilles is made into Belinda's large petticoat, and the **epic** battle of Homeric poetry becomes a card game in Pope's mock-heroic treatment. Pope treats the whole conflict arising from the incident as if it were some mighty struggle between the Greeks and the Trojans, with ironic and sometimes ludicrous results.

Yet it should be remembered that by fitting such classical conventions into an Augustan setting, Pope was fulfilling the dual function of poking fun both at 18th Century society and the classics. From beginning to end, the entire poem maintains the lofty tone of **epic** poetry while never losing touch with its mock-heroic purpose. Probably the best example of Pope's handling of

epic machinery is to be found in his use of the sylphs. One of the great traditions of **epic** poetry was the introduction of the gods, who became deeply involved in the affairs of mortals, guarding them and even punishing them according to the needs of the tale. Pope took this tradition and molded it into the Augustan pattern by changing the omnipotent gods into delightfully minute spirits called sylphs. The sylphs were not included in the 1712 edition, and it stands as a tribute to the poet's craftsmanship that their inclusion in the 1714 version improved the poem by completing the all-around satirical effect. Pope also borrowed ideas from other sources and merged them into his satirical use of **epic** conventions. At one point in the poem, for example, he talks of the sylphs in military terms, recalling the traditional way of regarding the gods. Also, the heroes of Western European literature were often assigned gods as personal guardians, and Pope draws on this idea when he makes the sylphs Belinda's protectors. There was another ancient tradition whereby the souls of the dead were turned into spirits who guarded their living friends. Pope brings this conception into Ariel's speech to Belinda in Canto I.

It is interesting as well to note the various resemblances between Pope's Ariel and the character of the same name in Shakespeare's play. The sylphs are also involved in various antics which are obviously meant to mimic the activities of the angels in Milton's *Paradise Lost*. It can be seen, then, that Pope not only obeyed Le Bossu's rule concerning classical **conventions** in mock-epic poetry, but also developed the established traditions to a degree of craftsmanship which has never been surpassed in this type of verse. *The Rape of the Lock* displays both old **conventions** and fresh conceptions fused into one harmonious whole.

Question: What does this poem tell us about Pope's character, attitude to society, view of life and stature as a poet?

Answer: Because of his religion and deformity, Pope developed a very bitter attitude toward his fellow men, which revealed itself most pointedly in his famous poem, *The Dunciad*. He was only twenty-four when he wrote *The Rape of the Lock*, however, and although his **satire** is sharp, the poem displays none of the personal bitterness that crept into his later work. It shows Pope, in fact, to be a man uncommon charm with a sparkling sense of humor marked by kindness and sympathy. He also comes through as someone sustained by an attitude of honesty and integrity, particularly in his views on contemporary society. In this respect, we must not forget that Pope was not yet fully established as a famous poet, and that he courted a great deal of disfavor by ridiculing statesmen, nobles, and royalty. It should also be remembered that by satirizing so many aspects of society, Pope was exposing his own self to the possibility of attack and ridicule - and he was indeed an easy target. Personal courage is a quality for which the poet, in view of his physical, social and religious handicaps, has not been praised nearly enough.

It cannot honestly be said, however, that this poem shows his general view of life to have been a particularly wide or generous one, inasmuch as it deals with only one facet of society - the elegant, upper-class one. Pope moved in these circles, of course, and we get practically no idea from this poem that any other kind of society existed. While the Augustans believed that, in Pope's words, "The proper study of Mankind is Man," the impression one receives from this poem is that only men of taste and elegance are being studied. We must never forget that everything Pope wrote adhered strictly to the rules of his age. While this had a certain restrictive effect on style and vision, his greatness really lies in what he did within that limited context. In this poem Pope achieved a controlled fluidity of style and facile treatment of **theme** which mark him as an outstanding

Augustan craftsman. Translated into French and Italian, *The Rape of the Lock* immediately established him as a major poet, and with his translations of Homer's *Iliad* and *Odyssey*, his reputation and fortune were assured. In judging Pope's stature as a poet, with this mock-heroic poem as a guide, we must take into account not only the literary bounds within which he worked, but also the purpose he had in writing it in the first place. His aim was to settle a quarrel by writing a poem which would expose the ludicrous nature of the dispute and which would also encompass many features of 18th Century life that Pope found to be equally ludicrous.

The poem has been attacked as a shallow, frivolous work, but this is not so; it is a lighthearted piece of fun brilliantly executed within a neoclassical framework. It succeeds rather in attacking the shallowness and frivolity of contemporary society by taking a tongue-in-cheek attitude to the most absurd incidents - and people. Pope did not intend this to be a profound work, and he maintains a lighthearted atmosphere throughout. It can also be said that it is in a very real sense a work in which sincere values are advocated, not positively (apart from Clarissa's speech) but by ridiculing the insincerities and lack of values all too prevalent in upper-class Augustan society.

Question: Discuss the poem as an example of the mock-heroic tradition in literature.

Answer: At the beginning of his Dedication, Pope describes the poem as "heroi-comical," thus consciously placing it within the tradition of mock-heroic literature. In European literature, this tradition goes right back to the ancient Greeks themselves. Two methods of approach were laid down in those days, whereby trivial incidents and insignificant details were treated in an inflated way, and great events were reduced to ludicrous proportions. These techniques continued to dominate satirical writing as late as the 16th Century, when Vida's poem *A Game of Chess* was written, the 17th Century, when Tassoni's work *The Rape of the Bucket* was produced, and the 18th Century, in which mock-heroic poetry reached its peak with *The Rape of the Lock*. Pope borrowed ideas and skills from these earlier works, but his poem is outstanding for the way in which all the mock-epic elements are developed and blended.

We must remember, however, that this mock-heroic tradition had set rules and regulations which, in the true Augustan tradition, had to be obeyed. These rules were itemized by a 17th Century French critic called Le Bossu, who said that poetry of this kind had to contain as many classical epic devices as possible, that it must contain samples of **epic** "machinery," and that it had to have a single action which takes place in the poet's homeland. Pope's poem is therefore totally **epic** in tone, contains mock-epic battle scenes, mimics the mythical gods, and is contemporary in its setting. It also follows Le Bossu's regulations by being thoroughly **didactic**, setting out to teach society a sharp lesson in conduct and ethical standards. The poem achieves this by such methods as treating Belinda's "Toilette" as a religious ritual, or turning the noble type of Greek hero into a mincing Augustan fop. But the two writers who most influenced Pole's thinking on mock-heroic poetry were a French-man called Boileau and an Englishman called Garth. Boileau's great poem, *Le Lutrin*, sustains a strong moral tone, and this prompted Pope to insert Clarissa's speech in Canto V. Pope also borrowed from the Frenchman the idea of ridiculing currently modish literature-French Romances, and the Atlantis for example, and received from him the idea of giving the fight between Belinda and the Baron an absurd ending. Although as an example of mock-heroic poetry, Garth's *The Dispensary* is a relatively mediocre work, it nevertheless prompted Pope to improve *The Rape of the Lock* in two respects. In the first place, the idea of combining something one line comes from Garth. Secondly, Garth's insistence on making ironic comments on fashionable society inspired Pope to write such passages as the description of Belinda's boudoir in Canto I.

It should be stressed, however, that Pope's poem stands unequalled as an example of mock-heroic verse. In obeying Le Bossu's rules, he surpasses them; in borrowing ideas from Vida and Tassoni, he improves upon them; in receiving ideas from Boileau and Garth, he embellishes them beyond recognition. Pope in fact took the best elements from the mock-heroic tradition and did things with them that no other poet has been able to do in this medium. His **irony** is subtle, his attack is powerful but controlled, and his, "wit" is exemplary.

Question: Write a brief essay on the structure, characterization, and historical background of the poem.

Answer: Written in 1711, the first version of Pope's poem was published in 1712, and consisted of two cantos. Although this poem can stand on its own merit, Pope was dissatisfied with it because it did not fulfill all the aims of mock-heroic poetry. This was due to the absence of **allusions** to the epic "machinery" of the gods, and in the 1714 edition this was remedied by the inclusion of the sylphs. In 1717 one more major addition was made in the form of Clarissa's speech, which was included to heighten the moral tone of the poem. Pope has been criticized for this addition on the grounds that it is superfluous and too serious compared to the rest of the poem. On the other hand, he deserves the highest praise for the very conception of the sylphs, and for the brilliant way he blends them into the structure of the poem without making them obtrusive. The main argument against the 1714 version is that it is unbalanced and unwieldy compared to the earlier edition. When one takes into consideration all the aspects of society and **epic** poetry that are successfully satirized in *The Rape of the Lock*, however, this criticism is completely invalid.

In any discussion of Pope's characterization in this poem, it should be born in mind that the poet was poking fun at types as well as individuals. Belinda is not only Arabella Fermor-she is also the personification of the 18th Century belle. Sir Plume represents the typical Augustan dandy as well as Sir George Browne. In addition, of course, his people are absurd versions of the central figures in classical epics, and it is a remarkable fact that Pope succeeds in merging individuals and types into literary characters who have their own individuality. The poem can really be examined as a neoclassic poetic portrait of Augustan society, with the beaux, belles and sylphs springing to life for us through Pope's evocative **imagery** and subtle implications. Yes it would be wrong to say that the poet **burlesques** his characters in this poem. **Burlesque** is indeed used-in Sir Plume's use of slang during the fight, for example, or in Belinda's hysterics after the removal of the lock - but his figures always retain a certain dignity which prevents the poem from descending to cheap mockery. *The Rape of the Lock* was written with a sense of humor and sympathy rather than in a mood of contempt and hostility.

Since the poem was written to reconcile two contemporary families, the Fermors and the Petres, it should be read with its historical background in mind. It was very well received in the poet's day, being translated into French and Italian, and bringing him international recognition as a major poet. From the historical point of view alone, it is an interesting work to study, inasmuch as it mirrors so much of the age, reflecting its faults while giving us a glance at its virtues. All the polished elegance and ludicrous vanities of the Augustan Age are exposed for us her while Pope succeeds in giving his **satire** the necessary touch of universality to make it ageless. Although the customs, dress, speech, and habits of modern society have very little in common with those of the 18th Century, we can still see many of the same social foibles around us that Pope saw in his day. The human failings which were satirized in ancient Greece and 18th Century England are not totally absent today.

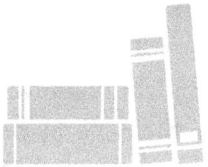

THE RAPE OF THE LOCK TO OTHER WORKS

ESSAY QUESTIONS AND ANSWERS

Question: To what extent would you say *Windsor Forest* and the *Pastorals* are Augustan poems?

Answer: These poems are Augustan inasmuch as they fulfill many 18th Century demands as far as **rhyme** scheme, form and content go. As we have seen, this was not an age in which nature, in the sense of trees, flowers and so on, was admired very much. It was an urban civilization in which elegance, taste and wit were to be sought after in all things, including poetry. "Nature" - in the 18th Century sense - had to be "methodized" in order to make it more beautiful and perfect, so when Pope set about to write these two poems he bore this in mind. Compared to, say, the poems of Wordsworth, they are not successful as evocative, lyrical descriptions of scenic beauty, because they lack the kind of exciting abandon which characterizes the best in romantic poetry. If we consider the poems in their historical setting, however, they may well be regarded as bold experiments by a youthful and ambitious Augustan. *Windsor Forest* in particular contains some beautiful descriptive passages with more color and fire than we expect from an 18th Century poet. Pope does not succeed in developing the historical aspects of the poem, however, and overloads the second part with almost absurd flattery. The *Pastorals* are typically Augustan imitations of the classical eclogues, but when translated into an 18th Century English setting, the **theme** and tone become somewhat strained and unnatural. The scenery here is like something painted on a flimsy canvas, and the characters come through as lisping Augustan fops.

Question: Does *Eloisa to Abelard* succeed in capturing all the dramatic elements of the original story?

Answer: The **theme** of this story is love, but it is a love of a unique kind. The tension is created not by Eloisa's desire for Abelard set against her love for God, but is caused rather by her knowledge that she is spiritually committed to the religious life while emotionally bound to her lover. Pope captures this mood effectively, although there is a definite feeling of his "holding back" in the passages which should thrill us with their poignant expressions of passion and frustration. Here again Pope is a victim of the limitations of his age, in which unbridled outpourings of personal emotion were frowned upon. Nevertheless, when we compare Pope's poetic rendition of this story with the Hughes prose translation of Eloisa's epistle, we can see that in many ways he avoided the worst features of 18th Century conventions. He does not make the story ludicrous, for example, by portraying Eloisa as a languishing, cloistered belle and Abelard a lisping, tonsured beau. He certainly succeeds in retaining much of the medieval atmosphere, and in so doing avoids the obvious pitfalls which Augustan poetry often fell into. The use of the heroic **couplet** for such a **theme** does not improve the poem, however, and the neat, polished effect is somehow or other out of place in such an emotional framework. It can be said that Pope does capture the dramatic effects of the story to a greater extent than one would expect in an Augustan, though the poem lacks the intensity which the **theme** demands.

Question: Would you say that Pope was successful as a critic of poetry and of man?

Answer: Pope turned to the classics and the Continent to a great extent for his ideas on criticism. The 18th Century was, of course, the age of neoclassicism, in which Homer was read with particular fervor, but it was also the time when English writers looked to the Continent for literary models and critical concepts. Pope admired Homer tremendously, particularly for his ability to "invent," and also made a close study of the great French critic, Le Bossu. Pope showed himself to be a critic in his own right, however, by attacking Le Bossu's opinion that rules and regulations had to be firmly established first before a poet could write. Learning and genius were, according to Pope, the prerequisites of poetic endeavor. "Imitation" to him meant not merely the slavish adaptation of a foreign work into one's own language, but rather the borrowing of the best ideas and concepts, and the molding of them into one's own tradition. This was the true mark of Augustan humanism, whereby contemporary man was studied and analyzed in the light of the best classical tradition. In this respect, too, Pope had his own ideas, which he outlined in his *Essay on Man*. Although this poem is unsuccessful philosophically inasmuch as it does not develop one central idea to a definitive conclusion, it nevertheless outlines in abrupt pronouncements the high standards of morality which Pope deemed essential to man's happiness. In his writings on poetry and on man, Pope shows no profound intellectual insights, but he does outline fresh ideas with the controlled, poised ease typical of his age.

BIBLIOGRAPHY

Social Background

Allen, R. J., *Life in Eighteenth-Century England*, 1941.

Besant, W., *London in the Eighteenth Century*, 1902.

George, M. D., *English Social Life in the Eighteenth Century*, 1923.

Turberville, A. S., *English Men and Manners in the Eighteenth Century*, 1926.

General Criticism and Interpretation

Butt, J., *The Augustan Age*, 1950.

Clifford, J. L., and Landa, L. A., eds., *Pope and His Contemporaries*. Essays presented to George Sherburn, 1949.

Elto, O., *The Augustan Age*, 1899.

Humphreys, A. R., *The Augustan World. Life and Letters in Eighteenth-Century England*, 1954.

McCutcheon, R. P., *Eighteenth-Century English Literature*, 1950.

Saintsbury, G., *The Peace of the Augustans*, 1916.

Vines, S., *The Course of English Classicism*, 1930.

Poetry

Brown, W. C., *The Triumph of Form. A Study of the Later Masters of the Heroic Couplet*, 1948.

Doughty, O., *English Lyric in the Age of Reason*, 1922.

Good, C. M., *Horace in the English Literature of the Eighteenth Century*, 1918.

Jack, I., *Augustan* Satire, 1660-1750, 1952.

Lowes, J. L., Convention *and Revolt in Poetry*, 1919.

Smith, D. Nichol, *Some Observations on Eighteenth-Century Poetry*, 1937.

Sutherland, J. R., *A Preface to Eighteenth-Century Poetry*, 1948.

Criticism And Theory

Bate, W. J., *From Classic to Romantic*, 1946.

Bosker, A., *Literary Criticism in the Age of Johnson*, 1930; rev. 1954.

Empson, W., "Wit in the Essay on Criticism" in *The Structure of Complex Works*, 1951.

Herrick, M. T., *The Poetics of Aristotle in England*, 1930.

Needham, H. A., ed., *Taste and Criticism in the Eighteenth Century*, 1952.

Alexander Pope

Brower, A. B., *Alexander Pope: The Poetry of* Allusion, 1959.

Edwards, T. R., *This Dark Estate*, 1963.

Knight, G. W., *Laureate of Peace*, 1955.

Mack, Maynard, *Essential Articles for the Study of Alexander Pope*, 1964.

Parkin Rebecca, *The Poetic Workmanship*, 1955.

Tillotson, G., *Alexander Pope: The Rape of the Lock*, 1942.

Tillotson, G., *On the Poetry of Pope*, 1950.

Tillotson, G., *Pope and Human Nature*, 1958.

Ward, Sir A. W., *The Poetical Works of Pope*, 1961.

www.ingramcontent.com/pod-product-compliance
Lightning Source LLC
LaVergne TN
LVHW011709060526
838200LV00051B/2831